用心雕刻每一本......

http://site.douban.com/110283/
http://weibo.com/nccpub

用心字里行间　雕刻名著经典

Business Ethics and Social Responsibility

Tenth Edition

O.C. Ferrell
University of New Mexico

Geoffrey A. Hirt
DePaul University

Linda Ferrell
University of New Mexico

商业伦理与社会责任

第 10 版

双语教学版

O.C. 费雷尔
[美] 杰弗里·赫特 著
琳达·费雷尔

人民邮电出版社
北 京

图书在版编目（CIP）数据

商业伦理与社会责任：第 10 版：双语教学版 /（美）O.C. 费雷尔，（美）杰弗里·赫特，（美）琳达·费雷尔著 . -- 北京：人民邮电出版社，2018.3

商务英语 / 工商管理双语教学教材系列

ISBN 978-7-115-47607-4

Ⅰ . ①商… Ⅱ . ① O… ②杰… ③琳… Ⅲ . ①商业道德—双语教学—教材—汉、英 Ⅳ . ① F718

中国版本图书馆 CIP 数据核字（2018）第 004637 号

O.C. Ferrell, Geoffrey A. Hirt, Linda Ferrell

Business Ethics and Social Responsibility, 10th Edition

ISBN 978-1-259-17939-6

商业伦理与社会责任（第 10 版，双语教学版）

◆ 著 ［美］O.C. 费雷尔 杰弗里·赫特 琳达·费雷尔
策 划 刘 力 陆 瑜
责任编辑 李 丹
装帧设计 陶建胜

◆ 人民邮电出版社出版发行 北京市丰台区成寿寺路 11 号
邮编 100164 电子邮件 315@ptpress.com.cn
网址 http://www.ptpress.com.cn
电话（编辑部）010-84937150 （市场部）010-84937152
三河市少明印务有限公司印刷
新华书店经销

◆ 开本：850 × 1092 1 /16
印张：8.25
字数：210 千字
2018 年 3 月第 1 版 2018 年 3 月第 1 次印刷

定价：38.00 元

本书如有印装质量问题，请与本社联系 电话：(010) 84937150

内容提要

《商业伦理与社会责任》（第 10 版，双语教学版）摘编自 *Business: A Changing World*（10e）一书，该书是美国同类书市场领导品牌。第一作者 O.C. 费雷尔教授，曾担任美国营销协会学术委员会主席，其研究领域包括全球商业、市场营销和商业伦理。本书主要讲述在当今商业世界的快速变化中的商业伦理与社会责任，具体内容包括企业的本质，经济学的基本知识，商学学习的框架体系，商业伦理与社会责任在企业决策中的作用，国家间进行贸易的障碍与推动因素，国际贸易中企业的参与形式及跨国教育的策略。本书保留了原版书中全部的英文及其教材要素，编者对目录以及部分专业词汇进行了翻译。书中还引用了一些新鲜有趣的商业案例、习题，语言简练，通俗易懂。

本书可作为高等院校财经类及商务英语专业的双语课适用教材，也适用于 MBA 学员、企业管理者以及对该领域有兴趣的普通读者。

Authors 作者简介

O.C. FERRELL

O.C. Ferrell is University Distinguished Professor of Marketing and Bill Daniels Professor of Business Ethics in the Anderson School of Management at the University of New Mexico. He served as the Bill Daniels Distinguished Professor of Business Ethics at the University of Wyoming and the Chair of the Department of Marketing at Colorado State University. He also has held faculty positions at the University of Memphis, University of Tampa, Texas A&M University, Illinois State University, and Southern Illinois University, as well as visiting positions at Queen's University (Ontario, Canada), University of Michigan (Ann Arbor), University of Wisconsin (Madison), and University of Hannover (Germany). He has served as a faculty member for the Master's Degree Program in Marketing at Thammasat University (Bangkok, Thailand). Dr. Ferrell received his B.A. and M.B.A. from Florida State University and his Ph.D. from Louisiana State University. His teaching and research interests include business ethics, global business, and marketing.

Dr. Ferrell is widely recognized as a leading teacher and scholar in business. He has published more than 100 articles in leading journals. He has co-authored more than 20 books. In addition to *Business: A Changing World,* he has two other textbooks, *Marketing* and *Business Ethics: Ethical Decision Making and Cases,* that are market leaders in their respective areas. He also has co-authored other textbooks for marketing, management, business and society, and other business courses, as well as a trade book on business ethics. He chaired the American Marketing Association (AMA) ethics committee that developed its current code of ethics. He is past president of the Academic Council for the AMA. Currently he is Vice President of Publications for the Academy of Marketing Science and is a Distinguished Fellow with AMS and is the AMS, Cutco-Vector Distinguished Marketing Educator.

Dr. Ferrell's major focus is teaching and developing teaching resources for students and faculty to better understand the increasing complex global business environment. He has taught the introduction to business course using this textbook. This gives him the opportunity to develop, improve, and test the book and ancillary materials on a firsthand basis. He has traveled extensively to work with students and understands the needs of instructors of introductory business courses. He lives in Albuquerque, New Mexico, and enjoys skiing, golf, and international travel.

GEOFFREY A. HIRT

Geoffrey A. Hirt of DePaul University previously taught at Texas Christian University and Illinois State University where he was Chairman of the Department of Finance and Law. At DePaul, he was Chairman of the Finance Department from 1987 to 1997 and held the title of Mesirow Financial Fellow. He developed the MBA program in Hong Kong and served as Director of International Initiatives for the College of Business, supervising overseas programs in Hong Kong, Prague, and Manama and was awarded the Spirit of St. Vincent DePaul award for his contributions to the university. Dr. Hirt directed the Chartered Financial Analysts (CFA) study program for the Investment Analysts Society of Chicago from 1987 to 2003. He has been a visiting professor at the University of Urbino in Italy, where he still maintains a relationship with the economics department. He received his Ph.D. in Finance from the University of Illinois at Champaign–Urbana, his M.B.A. at Miami University of Ohio, and his B.A. from Ohio Wesleyan University.

Dr. Hirt is currently on the Dean's Advisory Board and Executive Committee of DePaul's School of Music and is on the Board of the James Tyree Foundation. The Tyree Foundation funds innovative education programs in Chicago, and Dr. Hirt also serves on the Grant Committee. Dr. Hirt is past president and a current member of the Midwest Finance Association, a former editor of the *Journal of Financial Education,* and also a member of the Financial Management Association. He belongs to the Pacific Pension Institute, an organization of public pension funds, private equity firms, and international organizations such as the Asian Development Bank, the IMF, and the European Bank for Reconstruction and Development.

Dr. Hirt is widely known for his textbook *Foundations of Financial Management* published by McGraw-Hill/Irwin. This book in its fifteenth edition has been used in more than 31 countries and translated into more than 14 different languages. Additionally, Dr. Hirt is well known for his textbook, *Fundamentals of Investment Management,* also published by McGraw-Hill/Irwin and now in its tenth edition. Dr. Hirt enjoys golf, swimming, music, and traveling with his wife, who is a pianist and opera coach.

LINDA FERRELL

Dr. Linda Ferrell is Professor of Marketing and Bill Daniels Professor of Business Ethics in the Anderson School of Management at the University of New Mexico. She completed her Ph.D. in Business Administration, with a concentration in management, at the University of Memphis. She has taught at the University of Tampa, Colorado State University, University of Northern Colorado, University of Memphis, and the University of Wyoming. She also team teaches a class at Thammasat University in Bangkok, Thailand, as well as an online Business Ethics Certificate course through the University of New Mexico.

Her work experience as an account executive for McDonald's and Pizza Hut's advertising agencies supports her teaching of advertising, marketing management, marketing ethics, and marketing principles. She has published in the *Journal of Public Policy & Marketing, Journal of Business Research, Journal of the Academy of Marketing Science, Journal of Business Ethics, AMS Review, Journal of Academic Ethics, Journal of Marketing Education, Marketing Education Review, Journal of Teaching Business Ethics,* and *Case Research Journal,* and is co-author of *Business Ethics: Ethical Decision Making and Cases* (10th edition) and *Business and Society* (5th edition). She co-leads the Daniels Fund business ethics initiative at the University of New Mexico.

Dr. Ferrell is the President of the Academy of Marketing Science and a past president for the Marketing Management Association. She is a member of the college advisory board for Cutco Vector. She is on the NASBA Center for the Public Trust Board of Directors, University of Central Florida-Nicholson School of Communication Board of Visitors, University of Tampa-Sykes College of Business, Board of Fellows, and the Direct Selling Education Foundation Board and Executive Committee. She frequently speaks to organizations on "Teaching Business Ethics," including the Direct Selling Education Foundation's training programs, Ethics & Compliance Officer Association, NASBA Center for the Public Trust Ethical Leadership Conference, as well as others. She has served as an expert witness in cases related to advertising, business ethics, and consumer protection.

Contents 目录

Business Ethics and Social Responsibility

1 The Dynamics of Business and Economics

商业与经济的动力

Learning Objectives

After reading this chapter, you will be able to:

- **LO 1-1** Define basic concepts such as business, product, and profit.
- **LO 1-2** Identify the main participants and activities of business and explain why studying business is important.
- **LO 1-3** Define economics and compare the four types of economic systems.
- **LO 1-4** Describe the role of supply, demand, and competition in a free-enterprise system.
- **LO 1-5** Specify why and how the health of the economy is measured.
- **LO 1-6** Trace the evolution of the American economy and discuss the role of the entrepreneur in the economy.
- **LO 1-7** Evaluate a small-business owner's situation and propose a course of action.

Chapter Outline

进入商业世界

Enter the World of Business

竞争有益于企业

Competition Is Good for Business

Mattel vs. Hasbro, Microsoft vs. Apple, Walmart vs. Target—the battles between these competitors are well known. Competition can be a strong motivator for business success. In a capitalist society, competition leads businesses to innovate and take risks. It is not uncommon for two or three key players to dominate an industry. These players often battle one another to provide the best product or experience for a customer, making it harder for new entrants to come in. It is essential that a business carefully monitor the progress of its primary competitor to maintain market share. However, sometimes the rivalry between businesses is so strong that their entire focus is on destroying the competition. When this occurs, businesses can fail to consider the threat of newer entrants and even face legal consequences because of anticompetitive actions.

Perhaps one of the largest business rivalries is between Coca-Cola and Pepsi. Seven years after Coca-Cola was launched, Pepsi was released. The two companies quickly became rivals, battling for shelf space and their quest to become the beverage of choice for consumers. For years, these two players dominated the industry. However, as soda sales began to flatten, competitors emerged to take advantage of new trends. Red Bull, for instance, tapped into the energy drink market.

Unlike Coca-Cola and Pepsi, Red Bull is not known for its good taste. Perhaps for this reason, its threat to the two beverage makers appeared minimal. Yet with its focus and branding on extreme sports, Red Bull surpassed Pepsi in brand value. The drink is now the third most valuable brand in the industry, after Coca-Cola and Diet Coke. While rivalry is a strong motivator, businesses must not get distracted from the possibility of newer competitors.[1]

引言
Introduction

We begin our study of business in this chapter by examining the fundamentals of business and economics. First, we introduce the nature of business, including its goals, activities, and participants. Next, we describe the basics of economics and apply them to the United States economy. Finally, we establish a framework for studying business in this text.

企业的本质
The Nature of Business

LO 1-1

企业
business
individuals or organizations who try to earn a profit by providing products that satisfy people's needs

产品
product
a good or service with tangible and intangible characteristics that provide satisfaction and benefits

A **business** tries to earn a profit by providing products that satisfy people's needs. The outcomes of its efforts are **products** that have both tangible and intangible characteristics that provide satisfaction and benefits. When you purchase a product, you are buying the benefits and satisfaction you think the product will provide. A Subway sandwich, for example, may be purchased to satisfy hunger, while a Honda Accord may be purchased to satisfy the need for transportation and the desire to present a certain image.

Most people associate the word *product* with tangible goods—an automobile, computer, phone, coat, or some other tangible item. However, a product can also be a service, which occurs when people or machines provide or process something of value to customers. Dry cleaning, a checkup by a doctor, a performance by a basketball player—these are examples of services. Some services, such as Flickr, an online photo management and sharing application, do not charge a fee for use but obtain revenue from ads on their sites. A product can also be an idea. Accountants and attorneys, for example, generate ideas for solving problems.

企业的目标
The Goal of Business

盈利
profit
the difference between what it costs to make and sell a product and what a customer pays for it

非营利组织
nonprofit organizations
organizations that may provide goods or services but do not have the fundamental purpose of earning profits

The primary goal of all businesses is to earn a **profit,** the difference between what it costs to make and sell a product and what a customer pays for it. If a company spends $8.00 to manufacture, finance, promote, and distribute a product that it sells for $10.00, the business earns a profit of $2.00 on each product sold. Businesses have the right to keep and use their profits as they choose—within legal limits—because profit is the reward for the risks they take in providing products. Earning profits contributes to society by providing employment, which in turn provides money that is reinvested in the economy. In addition, profits must be earned in a responsible manner. Not all organizations are businesses, however. **Nonprofit organizations,** such as National Public Radio (NPR), Habitat for Humanity, and other charities and social causes, do not have the fundamental purpose of earning profits, although they may provide goods or services and engage in fund raising.

To earn a profit, a person or organization needs management skills to plan, organize, and control the activities of the business and to find and develop employees so that it can make products consumers will buy. A business also needs marketing expertise to learn what products consumers need and want and to develop, manufacture, price, promote, and distribute those products. Additionally, a business needs financial resources and skills to fund, maintain, and expand its operations. Other challenges for businesspeople include abiding by laws and government regulations; acting in an ethical and socially responsible manner; and adapting to economic, technological, political, and social changes. Even nonprofit organizations engage in management, marketing, and finance activities to help reach their goals.

To achieve and maintain profitability, businesses have found that they must produce quality products, operate efficiently, and be socially responsible and ethical in dealing with customers, employees, investors, government regulators, and the community.

Because these groups have a stake in the success and outcomes of a business, they are sometimes called **stakeholders.** Many businesses, for example, are concerned about how the production and distribution of their products affect the environment. Concerns about landfills becoming high-tech graveyards plague many electronics firms. Sprint became the first wireless company to institute a buyback program that encourages customers to turn in their used mobile devices in exchange for up to $300 in credit. The company cleans and updates the devices and sells them as refurbished phones at a lower cost. This initiative has reached developing markets because these devices are in high demand for an affordable price. Those devices that are unusable are sent to a certified third party for recycling. The Environmental Protection Agency has recognized the program as one of the best.[2] Others are concerned with promoting business careers among African American, Hispanic, and Native American students. The Diversity Pipeline Alliance is a network of national organizations that work toward preparing students and professionals of color for leadership and management in the 21st-century workforce. The Pipeline assists individuals in getting into the appropriate college, pursuing a career in business, or earning an advanced degree in business.[3] Other companies, such as Home Depot, have a long history of supporting natural disaster victims, relief efforts, and recovery.

Consumers are often willing to pay more for products they perceive as environmentally-friendly.

利益相关者
stakeholders
groups that have a stake in the success and outcomes of a business

企业的参与者和主要活动
The People and Activities of Business

Figure 1.1 shows the people and activities involved in business. At the center of the figure are owners, employees, and customers; the outer circle includes the primary business activities—management, marketing, and finance. Owners have to put up resources—money or credit—to start a business. Employees are responsible for the work that goes on within a business. Owners can manage the business themselves or hire employees to accomplish this task. The president, CEO, and chairman of the board of Procter & Gamble, A.G. Lafley, does not own P&G, but is an employee who is responsible for managing all the other employees in a way that earns a profit for investors, who are the real owners. Finally, and most importantly, a business's major role is to satisfy the customers who buy its goods or services. Note also that people and forces beyond an organization's control—such as legal and regulatory forces, the economy, competition, technology, the political environment, and ethical and social concerns—all have an impact on the daily operations of businesses. You will learn more about these participants in business activities throughout this book. Next, we will examine the major activities of business.

管理

Management. Notice that in Figure 1.1 management and employees are in the same segment of the circle. This is because management involves coordinating employees' actions to achieve the firm's goals, organizing people to work efficiently, and motivating them to achieve the business's goals. Yang Yuanqing, CEO of Lenovo, recognizes the importance of management to company success. Under his

FIGURE 1.1
Overview of the Business World

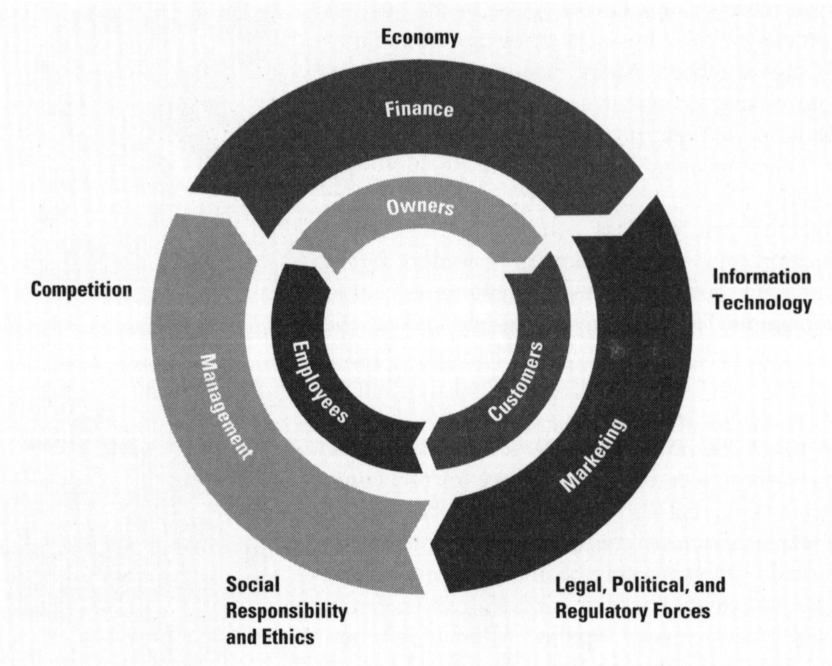

management, Lenovo has become one of the largest PC manufacturing businesses in the world, in addition to having a strong presence in other markets, such as mobile devices and servers. Their success is largely due to unique and efficient operations. All of the manufacturing activities are done in-house, allowing them to quickly adapt to changes in the market and consumer preferences.[4] Management is also concerned with acquiring, developing, and using resources (including people) effectively and efficiently. Amazon enlists workers and suppliers through its Vendor Flex Program to make distribution more efficient.[5]

Production and manufacturing is another element of management. Hershey, for example, invested $300 million in developing infrastructure and building a new manufacturing plant in Pennsylvania, which is equipped with production technology unprecedented in the candy industry. They are also extensively training 700 employees to manage the plant's operations.[6] In essence, managers plan, organize, staff, and control the tasks required to carry out the work of the company or nonprofit organization. We take a closer look at management activities in Parts 3 and 4 of this text.

市场营销

Marketing. Marketing and consumers are in the same segment of Figure 1.1 because the focus of all marketing activities is satisfying customers. Marketing includes all the activities designed to provide goods and services that satisfy consumers' needs and wants. Marketers gather information and conduct research to determine what customers want. Using information gathered from marketing research, marketers plan and develop products and make decisions about how much to charge for their products and when and where to make them available. They also analyze the marketing environment to see if products need to be modified. In response to First Lady Michelle Obama's campaign against childhood obesity, many companies announced they would begin offering products with reduced sugars, fats, and salts. Coca-Cola

The Aflac duck advertisement uses humor to demonstrate that Aflac focuses on the individual rather than the company.

has launched an anti-obesity campaign with videos encouraging people to be more active and promising to clearly label its products with calorie counts. Such a response could be a smart move on Coca-Cola's part because sodas are often viewed as a main contributor to obesity. Several companies, including ConAgra Foods, Bumble Bee Foods, and General Mills, have all committed to reducing calories in their products. As a result, they have eliminated 6.4 trillion calories from grocery shelves since 2009.[7] Marketers use promotion—advertising, personal selling, sales promotion (coupons, games, sweepstakes, movie tie-ins), and publicity—to communicate the benefits and advantages of their products to consumers and increase sales. Nonprofit organizations also use promotion. For example, the National Fluid Milk Processor Promotion Board's "milk mustache" advertising campaign has featured Brooke Shields, Beyoncé Knowles, Sheryl Crow, Elizabeth Hurley, Serena Williams, and even animated "celebrities" such as Garfield.[8] We will examine marketing activities in Part 5 of this text.

财务

Finance. Owners and finance are in the same part of Figure 1.1 because, although management and marketing have to deal with financial considerations, it is the primary responsibility of the owners to provide financial resources for the operation of the business. Moreover, the owners have the most to lose if the business fails to make a profit. Finance refers to all activities concerned with obtaining money and using it effectively. People who work as accountants, stockbrokers, investment advisors, or bankers are all part of the financial world. Owners sometimes have to borrow money from banks to get started or attract additional investors who become partners or stockholders. Owners of small businesses in particular often rely on bank loans for funding. Part 6 of this text discusses financial management.

为什么学习商学
Why Study Business?

Studying business can help you develop skills and acquire knowledge to prepare for your future career, regardless of whether you plan to work for a multinational *Fortune*

500 firm, start your own business, work for a government agency, or manage or volunteer at a nonprofit organization. The field of business offers a variety of interesting and challenging career opportunities throughout the world, such as marketing, human resources management, information technology, finance, production and operations, wholesaling and retailing, and many more.

Studying business can also help you better understand the many business activities that are necessary to provide satisfying goods and services—and that these activities carry a price tag. For example, if you buy a new compact disk, about half of the price goes toward activities related to distribution and the retailer's expenses and profit margins. The production (pressing) of the CD represents about $1, or a small percentage of its price. Most businesses charge a reasonable price for their products to ensure that they cover their production costs, pay their employees, provide their owners with a return on their investment, and perhaps give something back to their local communities. Bill Daniels founded Cablevision, building his first cable TV system in Casper, Wyoming, in 1953, and is now considered "the father of cable television." Prior to Daniels' passing in 2000, he had established a foundation that currently has funding of $1.1 billion and supports a diversity of causes from education to business ethics. During his career, Daniels created the Young Americans Bank, where children could create bank accounts and learn about financial responsibility, and this remains the world's only charter bank for young people. He created the Daniels College of Business through a donation of $20 million to the University of Denver. During his life, he affected many individuals and organizations, and his business success has allowed his legacy to be one of giving and impacting communities throughout the United States.[9] Thus, learning about business can help you become a well-informed consumer and member of society.

Business activities help generate the profits that are essential not only to individual businesses and local economies but also to the health of the global economy. Without profits, businesses find it difficult, if not impossible, to buy more raw materials, hire more employees, attract more capital, and create additional products that in turn make more profits and fuel the world economy. Understanding how our free-enterprise economic system allocates resources and provides incentives for industry and the workplace is important to everyone.

企业的经济基础
The Economic Foundations of Business

LO 1-3

To continue our introduction to business, it is useful to explore the economic environment in which business is conducted. In this section, we examine economic systems, the free-enterprise system, the concepts of supply and demand, and the role of competition. These concepts play important roles in determining how businesses operate in a particular society.

经济学
economics
the study of how resources are distributed for the production of goods and services within a social system

自然资源
natural resources
land, forests, minerals, water, and other things that are not made by people

人力资源
human resources
the physical and mental abilities that people use to produce goods and services; also called labor

Economics is the study of how resources are distributed for the production of goods and services within a social system. You are already familiar with the types of resources available. Land, forests, minerals, water, and other things that are not made by people are **natural resources. Human resources,** or labor, refer to the physical and mental abilities that people use to produce goods and services. **Financial resources,** or capital, are the funds used to acquire the natural and human resources needed to provide products. Because natural, human, and financial resources are used to produce goods and services, they are sometimes called *factors of production.* The firm can also have intangible resources such as a good reputation for quality products or being socially responsible. The goal is to turn the factors of production and intangible resources into a competitive advantage.

经济体制
Economic Systems

The Young Americans Bank in Denver was created by cable magnate Bill Daniels. It is the only chartered bank in the world that makes loans to children.

An **economic system** describes how a particular society distributes its resources to produce goods and services. A central issue of economics is how to fulfill an unlimited demand for goods and services in a world with a limited supply of resources. Different economic systems attempt to resolve this central issue in numerous ways, as we shall see.

Although economic systems handle the distribution of resources in different ways, all economic systems must address three important issues:

1. What goods and services, and how much of each, will satisfy consumers' needs?
2. How will goods and services be produced, who will produce them, and with what resources will they be produced?
3. How are the goods and services to be distributed to consumers?

Communism, socialism, and capitalism, the basic economic systems found in the world today (Table 1.1), have fundamental differences in the way they address these issues. The factors of production in command economies are controlled by government planning. In many cases, the government owns or controls the production of goods and services. Communism and socialism are, therefore, considered command economies.

共产主义
Communism. Karl Marx (1818–1883) first described **communism** as a society in which the people, without regard to class, own all the nation's resources. In his ideal political-economic system, everyone contributes according to ability and receives benefits according to need. In a communist economy, the people (through the government) own and operate all businesses and factors of production. Central government planning determines what goods and services satisfy citizens' needs, how the goods and services are produced, and how they are distributed.

财务资源
financial resources
the funds used to acquire the natural and human resources needed to provide products; also called capital

经济体制
economic system
a description of how a particular society distributes its resources to produce goods and services

共产主义
communism
first described by Karl Marx as a society in which the people, without regard to class, own all the nation's resources

TABLE 1.1
Comparison of Communism, Socialism, and Capitalism

	Communism	Socialism	Capitalism
Business ownership	Most businesses are owned and operated by the government.	The government owns and operates major industries; individuals own small businesses.	Individuals own and operate all businesses.
Competition	None. The government owns and operates everything.	Restricted in major industries; encouraged in small business.	Encouraged by market forces and government regulations.
Profits	Excess income goes to the government.	Profits earned by small businesses may be reinvested in the business; profits from government-owned industries go to the government.	Individuals are free to keep profits and use them as they wish.

Source: "Gross Domestic Product or Expenditure, 1930–2002".

社会主义
socialism
an economic system in which the government owns and operates basic industries but individuals own most businesses

社会主义
Socialism. **Socialism** is an economic system in which the government owns and operates basic industries—postal service, telephone, utilities, transportation, health care, banking, and some manufacturing—but individuals own most businesses. For example, in France the postal service industry La Poste is fully owned by the French government and makes a profit. Central planning determines what basic goods and services are produced, how they are produced, and how they are distributed. Individuals and small businesses provide other goods and services based on consumer demand and the availability of resources. Citizens are dependent on the government for many goods and services.

The Federal Trade Commission enforces antitrust laws and monitors businesses to ensure fair competition.

资本主义

Capitalism. **Capitalism,** or **free enterprise,** is an economic system in which individuals own and operate the majority of businesses that provide goods and services. Competition, supply, and demand determine which goods and services are produced, how they are produced, and how they are distributed. The United States, Canada, Japan, and Australia are examples of economic systems based on capitalism.

There are two forms of capitalism: pure capitalism and modified capitalism. In pure capitalism, also called a **free-market system,** all economic decisions are made without government intervention. This economic system was first described by Adam Smith in *The Wealth of Nations* (1776). Smith, often called the father of capitalism, believed that the "invisible hand of competition" best regulates the economy. He argued that competition should determine what goods and services people need. Smith's system is also called *laissez-faire* ("let it be") *capitalism* because the government does not interfere in business.

资本主义（自由企业制）
capitalism (free enterprise)
an economic system in which individuals own and operate the majority of businesses that provide goods and services

自由市场体系
free-market system
pure capitalism, in which all economic decisions are made without government intervention

Modified capitalism differs from pure capitalism in that the government intervenes and regulates business to some extent. One of the ways in which the United States and Canadian governments regulate business is through laws. Laws such as the Federal Trade Commission Act, which created the Federal Trade Commission to enforce antitrust laws, illustrate the importance of the government's role in the economy. In the most recent recession, the government provided loans and took ownership positions in banks such as Citigroup, AIG (an insurance company), and General Motors. These actions were thought necessary to keep these firms from going out of business and creating a financial disaster for the economy.

混合经济

Mixed Economies. No country practices a pure form of communism, socialism, or capitalism, although most tend to favor one system over the others. Most nations operate as **mixed economies,** which have elements from more than one economic system. In socialist Sweden, most businesses are owned and operated by private individuals. In capitalist United States, an independent federal agency operates the postal service and another independent agency operates the Tennessee Valley Authority, an electric utility. In Great Britain and Mexico, the governments are attempting to sell many state-run businesses to private individuals and companies. In Germany, the Deutsche Post is privatized and trades on the stock market. In once-communist

混合经济
mixed economies
economies made up of elements from more than one economic system

Russia, Hungary, Poland, and other eastern European nations, capitalist ideas have been implemented, including private ownership of businesses.

Countries such as Russia have used state capitalism to advance the economy. State capitalism tries to integrate the powers of the state with the advantages of capitalism. It is led by the government but uses capitalistic tools such as listing stateowned companies on the stock market and embracing globalization.[10] State capitalism includes some of the world's largest companies such as Russia's Gazprom, which is the largest natural gas company.

自由企业系统制度
The Free-Enterprise System

Many economies—including those of the United States, Canada, and Japan—are based on free enterprise, and many communist and socialist countries, such as China and Russia, are applying more principles of free enterprise to their own economic systems. Free enterprise provides an opportunity for a business to succeed or fail on the basis of market demand. In a free-enterprise system, companies that can efficiently manufacture and sell products that consumers desire will probably succeed. Inefficient businesses and those that sell products that do not offer needed benefits will likely fail as consumers take their business to firms that have more competitive products.

A number of basic individual and business rights must exist for free enterprise to work. These rights are the goals of many countries that have recently embraced free enterprise.

1. Individuals must have the right to own property and to pass this property on to their heirs. This right motivates people to work hard and save to buy property.
2. Individuals and businesses must have the right to earn profits and to use the profits as they wish, within the constraints of their society's laws, principles, and values.
3. Individuals and businesses must have the right to make decisions that determine the way the business operates. Although there is government regulation, the philosophy in countries like the United States and Australia is to permit maximum freedom within a set of rules of fairness.
4. Individuals must have the right to choose what career to pursue, where to live, what goods and services to purchase, and more. Businesses must have the right to choose where to locate, what goods and services to produce, what resources to use in the production process, and so on.

Without these rights, businesses cannot function effectively because they are not motivated to succeed. Thus, these rights make possible the open exchange of goods and services. In the countries that favor free enterprise, such as the United States, citizens have the freedom to make many decisions about the employment they choose and create their own productivity systems. Many entrepreneurs are more productive in free-enterprise societies because personal and financial incentives are available that can aid in entrepreneurial success. For many entrepreneurs, their work becomes a part of their system of goals, values, and lifestyle. Consider the panelists ("sharks") on the ABC program *Shark Tank.* Panelists on *Shark Tank* give entrepreneurs a chance to receive funding to realize their dreams by deciding whether to invest in their projects. They include Barbara Corcoran, who built one of New York's largest real estate companies; Mark Cuban, founder of Broadcast.com and MicroSolutions; and Daymond John, founder of clothing company FUBU.[11]

供给与需求的力量
The Forces of Supply and Demand

In the United States and in other free-enterprise systems, the distribution of resources and products is determined by supply and demand. **Demand** is the number of goods and services that consumers are willing to buy at different prices at a specific time. From your own experience, you probably recognize that consumers are usually willing to buy more of an item as its price falls because they want to save money. Consider handmade rugs, for example. Consumers may be willing to buy six rugs at $350 each, four at $500 each, but only two at $650 each. The relationship between the price and the number of rugs consumers are willing to buy can be shown graphically with a *demand curve* (see Figure 1.2).

需求
demand
the number of goods and services that consumers are willing to buy at different prices at a specific time

供给
supply
the number of products—goods and services—that businesses are willing to sell at different prices at a specific time

Supply is the number of products that businesses are willing to sell at different prices at a specific time. In general, because the potential for profits is higher, businesses are willing to supply more of a good or service at higher prices. For example, a company that sells rugs may be willing to sell six at $650 each, four at $500 each, but just two at $350 each. The relationship between the price of rugs and the quantity the company is willing to supply can be shown graphically with a *supply curve* (see Figure 1.2).

In Figure 1.2, the supply and demand curves intersect at the point where supply and demand are equal. The price at which the number of products that businesses are willing to supply equals the amount of products that consumers are willing to buy at a specific point in time is the **equilibrium price.** In our rug example, the company is willing to supply four rugs at $500 each, and consumers are willing to buy four rugs at $500 each. Therefore, $500 is the equilibrium price for a rug at that point in time, and most rug companies will price their rugs at $500. As you might imagine, a business that charges more than $500 (or whatever the current equilibrium price is) for its rugs will not sell many and might not earn a profit. On the other hand, a business that charges less than $500 accepts a lower profit per rug than could be made at the equilibrium price.

均衡价格
equilibrium price
the price at which the number of products that businesses are willing to supply equals the amount of products that consumers are willing to buy at a specific point in time

If the cost of making rugs goes up, businesses will not offer as many at the old price. Changing the price alters the supply curve, and a new equilibrium price results. This is an ongoing process, with supply and demand constantly changing in response to changes in economic conditions, availability of resources, and degree of competition. For example, the price of oil can change rapidly and has been between $35 and $145 a barrel over the last five years. Prices for goods and services vary according to these changes in supply and demand. This concept is the force that drives the distribution of resources (goods and services, labor, and money) in a free-enterprise economy.

Critics of supply and demand say the system does not distribute resources equally. The forces of supply and demand prevent sellers who have to sell at higher prices (because their costs are high) and buyers who cannot afford to buy goods at the equilibrium price from participating in the market. According to critics, the wealthy can

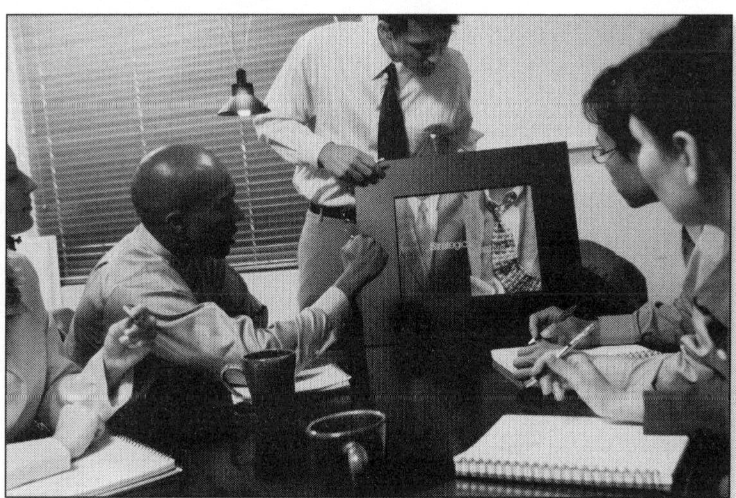

An entrepreneur presents his idea for a new product. Entrepreneurs are more productive in free-enterprise systems.

FIGURE 1.2
Equilibrium Price of Handmade Rugs

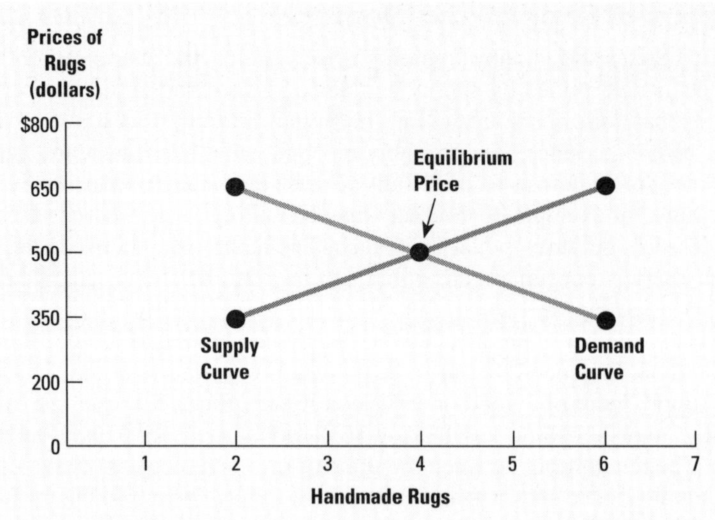

connect*

Need help understanding Supply and Demand? Visit your Connect ebook video tab for a brief animated explanation.

afford to buy more than they need, but the poor may be unable to buy enough of what they need to survive.

竞争的本质
The Nature of Competition

Competition, the rivalry among businesses for consumers' dollars, is another vital element in free enterprise. According to Adam Smith, competition fosters efficiency and low prices by forcing producers to offer the best products at the most reasonable price; those who fail to do so are not able to stay in business. Thus, competition should improve the quality of the goods and services available or reduce prices. Consider Marriott International, for example. It went from a small root beer stand in 1927 to its current status of 3,900 high-quality hotels in 72 countries. Marriott believed that if it treated its employees well, they in turn would provide good service to customers. Marriott has garnered a reputation as a high-quality hotel chain. It is now competing to attract younger travelers with reinvented lobbies filled with amenities and convenient ways to check in and out of a hotel, among other changes. It is also significantly expanding in Africa and Asia to capitalize on new market opportunities. The Marriott has been ranked as one of the leading hotel groups across the world. Competition and its drive to succeed have helped the firm achieve its current high status.[12]

竞争
competition
the rivalry among businesses for consumers' dollars

完全竞争
pure competition
the market structure that exists when there are many small businesses selling one standardized product

垄断竞争
monopolistic competition
the market structure that exists when there are fewer businesses than in a pure-competition environment and the differences among the goods they sell are small

Within a free-enterprise system, there are four types of competitive environments: pure competition, monopolistic competition, oligopoly, and monopoly.

Pure competition exists when there are many small businesses selling one standardized product, such as agricultural commodities like wheat, corn, and cotton. No one business sells enough of the product to influence the product's price. And, because there is no difference in the products, prices are determined solely by the forces of supply and demand.

Monopolistic competition exists when there are fewer businesses than in a pure-competition environment and the differences among the goods they sell is small. Aspirin, soft drinks, and vacuum cleaners are examples of such goods. These products differ slightly in packaging, warranty, name, and other characteristics, but all satisfy the same consumer need. Businesses have some power over the price they charge in

* 注：有需要 Connect 等在线资源的读者请致电麦格劳 – 希尔教育集团北京办公室 010–57997618。

Responding to Business Challenges

Swatch Works to Restructure Company, Supply Less Parts to Competition

The Swatch Group SA is known for its beautifully elegant watches as well as its high-quality and precisely made internal movements and components. These internal parts have generated many sales for the company. At the same time, it has also generated a number of challenges. For several years, Swatch has been appealing to the Swiss Competition Commission to change regulation under the Swiss Cartel Act. The act mandates that Swatch supply movements and components of watches to other watchmakers. In other words, Swatch must provide supplies to its competitors in the watch industry. Swatch wants to stop supplying components to its rivals. Being the main supplier increases Swatch's expenses while allowing its competition to invest more money in advertising, thus stifling Swatch's sales. Repeatedly, the company's requests have been delayed or declined by the Swiss government because of the large market share that Swatch has in the industry.

Swatch and its subsidiaries provide approximately 70 percent of the movements and 90 percent of components to other domestic and foreign brands. Stopping the supply will have a tremendous effect on the entire industry. While the Swiss government has agreed to minimal reductions in Swatch's supplying of movements, cuts to the supply of components cannot be reduced.[13]

Discussion Questions

1. Why does Swatch want to stop selling watch components?
2. Why is the Swiss government reluctant to allow Swatch to stop supplying components to its competitors?
3. Based on the large share of the watch movements and components industry that Swatch controls, which competitive environment do you think it operates in: pure competition, monopolistic competition, oligopoly, or monopoly?

---

monopolistic competition because they can make consumers aware of product differences through advertising. Jawbone, for example, differentiates its Jambox portable speakers through product design and quality. Consumers value some features more than others and are often willing to pay higher prices for a product with the features they want. For example, many consumers are willing to pay a higher price for organic fruits and vegetables rather than receive a bargain on nonorganic foods. The same holds true for non-genetically modified foods.

寡头
oligopoly
the market structure that exists when there are very few businesses selling a product

An **oligopoly** exists when there are very few businesses selling a product. In an oligopoly, individual businesses have control over their products' price because each business supplies a large portion of the products sold in the marketplace. Nonetheless, the prices charged by different firms stay fairly close because a price cut or increase by one company will trigger a similar response from another company. In the airline industry, for example, when one airline cuts fares to boost sales, other airlines quickly follow with rate decreases to remain competitive. On the other hand, airlines often raise prices at the same time. Oligopolies exist when it is expensive for new firms to enter the marketplace. Not just anyone can acquire enough financial capital to build an automobile production facility or purchase enough airplanes and related resources to build an airline.

完全垄断
monopoly
the market structure that exists when there is only one business providing a product in a given market

When there is one business providing a product in a given market, a **monopoly** exists. Utility companies that supply electricity, natural gas, and water are monopolies. The government permits such monopolies because the cost of creating the good or supplying the service is so great that new producers cannot compete for sales. Government-granted monopolies are subject to government-regulated prices. Some monopolies exist because of technological developments that are protected by patent laws. Patent laws grant the developer of new technology a period of time (usually 20 years) during which no other producer can use the same technology without the agreement of the original developer. The United States granted its first patent in 1790. Now its patent office receives hundreds of thousands of patent applications a year, although Asian countries—including Japan, China, and South Korea—are not far behind.[14] This monopoly allows the developer to recover research, development, and production expenses and to earn a reasonable profit. An example of this type of monopoly is the dry-copier process developed by Xerox. Xerox's patents have expired, however, and many imitators have forced market prices to decline.

经济扩张
economic expansion
the situation that occurs when an economy is growing and people are spending more money; their purchases stimulate the production of goods and services, which in turn stimulates employment

通货膨胀
inflation
a condition characterized by a continuing rise in prices

经济收缩
economic contraction
a slowdown of the economy characterized by a decline in spending and during which businesses cut back on production and lay off workers

经济衰退
recession
a decline in production, employment, and income

失业率
unemployment
the condition in which a percentage of the population wants to work but is unable to find jobs

经济周期和生产力
Economic Cycles and Productivity

扩张和收缩
Expansion and Contraction. Economies are not stagnant; they expand and contract. **Economic expansion** occurs when an economy is growing and people are spending more money. Their purchases stimulate the production of goods and services, which in turn stimulates employment. The standard of living rises because more people are employed and have money to spend. Rapid expansions of the economy, however, may result in **inflation,** a continuing rise in prices. Inflation can be harmful if individuals' incomes do not increase at the same pace as rising prices, reducing their buying power. The worst case of hyperinflation occurred in Hungary in 1946. At one point, prices were doubling every 15.6 hours. One of the most recent cases of hyperinflation occurred in Zimbabwe.[15] Zimbabwe suffered from hyperinflation so severe that its inflation percentage rate rose into the hundreds of millions. With the elimination of the Zimbabwean dollar and certain price controls, the inflation rate began to decrease, but not before the country's economy was virtually decimated.[16]

Economic contraction occurs when spending declines. Businesses cut back on production and lay off workers, and the economy as a whole slows down. Contractions of the economy lead to **recession**—a decline in production, employment, and income. Recessions are often characterized by rising levels of **unemployment,** which is measured as the percentage of the population that wants to work but is unable to find jobs. Figure 1.3 shows the overall unemployment rate in the civilian labor force over the past 80 years. Rising unemployment levels tend to stifle demand for

FIGURE 1.3 Annual Average Unemployment Rate, Civilian Labor Force, 16 Years and Over

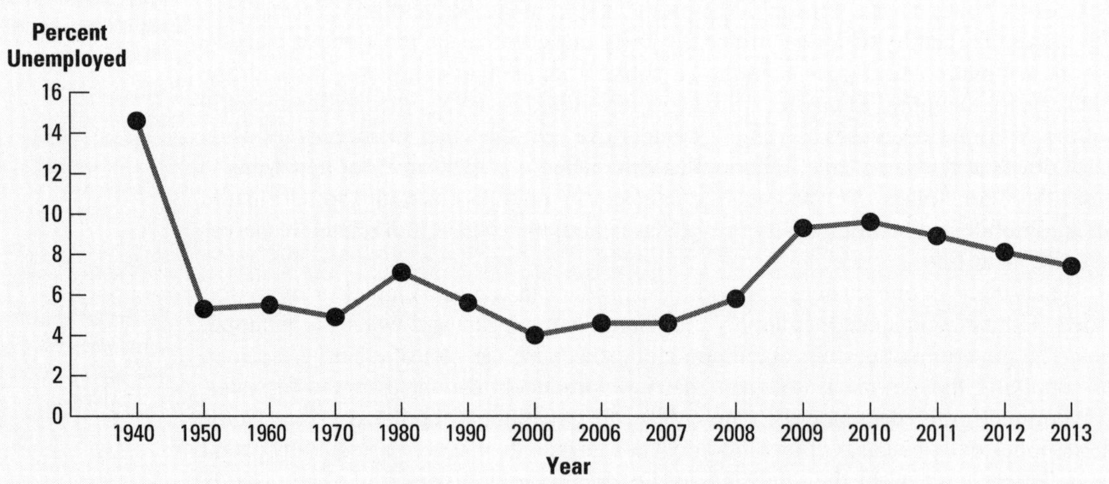

Sources: Bureau of Labor Statistics, "Household Data Annual Averages"; Bureau of Labor Statistics, "Labor Force Statistics from the Current Population Survey.

You can see what the U.S. government currently owes—down to the penny—by going to the website for the Bureau of the Public Debt.

goods and services, which can have the effect of forcing prices downward, a condition known as *deflation.* The United States has experienced numerous recessions, the most recent ones occurring in 1990–1991, 2002–2003, and 2008–2011. The most recent recession (or economic slowdown) was caused by the collapse in housing prices and consumers' inability to stay current on their mortgage and credit card payments. This caused a crisis in the banking industry, with the government bailing out banks to keep them from failing. This in turn caused a slowdown in spending on consumer goods and an increase in employment. Unemployment reached 10 percent of the labor force. Don't forget that personal consumption makes up almost 70 percent of gross domestic product, so consumer behavior is extremely important for economic activity. A severe recession may turn into a **depression,** in which unemployment is very high, consumer spending is low, and business output is sharply reduced, such as what occurred in the United States in the early 1930s. The most recent recession is often called the Great Recession because it was the longest and most severe economic decline since the Great Depression.

经济萧条
depression
a condition of the economy in which unemployment is very high, consumer spending is low, and business output is sharply reduced

Economies expand and contract in response to changes in consumer, business, and government spending. War also can affect an economy, sometimes stimulating it (as in the United States during World Wars I and II) and sometimes stifling it (as during the Vietnam, Persian Gulf, and Iraq wars). Although fluctuations in the economy are inevitable and to a certain extent predictable, their effects—inflation and unemployment—disrupt lives and thus governments try to minimize them.

衡量经济

Measuring the Economy. Countries measure the state of their economies to determine whether they are expanding or contracting and whether corrective action is necessary to minimize the fluctuations. One commonly used measure is **gross domestic product (GDP)**—the sum of all goods and services produced in a country during a year. GDP measures only those goods and services made within a country and therefore does not include profits from companies' overseas operations; it does include profits earned by foreign companies within the country being measured. However, it does not take into account the concept of GDP in relation to population (GDP per capita). Figure 1.4 shows the increase in GDP over several years, while Table 1.2 compares a number of economic statistics for a sampling of countries.

LO 1-5

国内生产总值
gross domestic product (GDP)
the sum of all goods and services produced in a country during a year

FIGURE 1.4
Growth in U.S. Gross Domestic Product

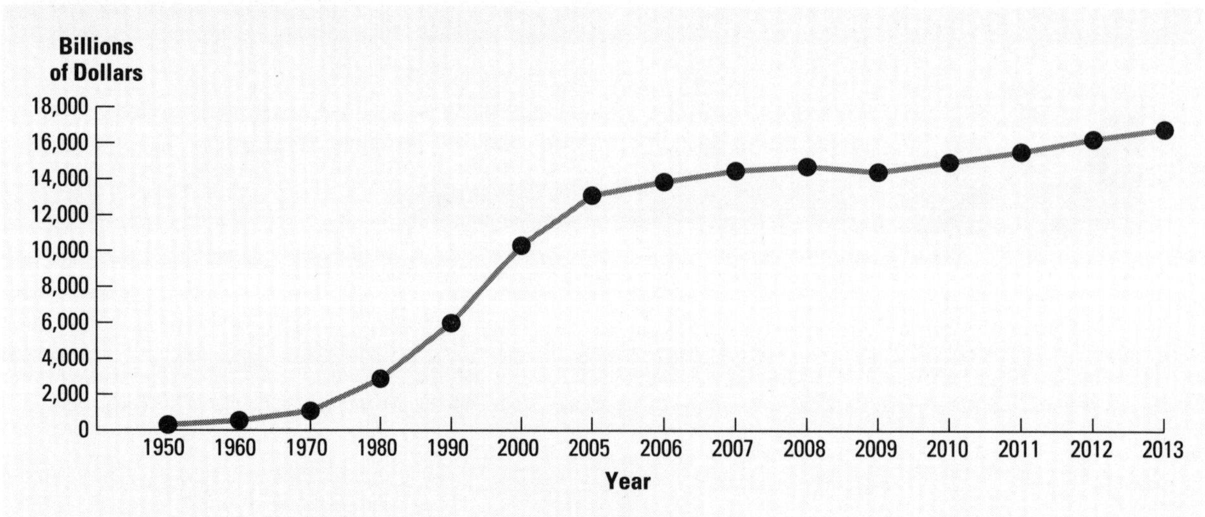

Source: U.S. Department of Commerce Bureau of Economic Analysis, "National Economic Accounts".

TABLE 1.2
Economic Indicators of Different Countries

Country	GDP (in billions of dollars)	GDP per Capita	Unemployment Rate (%)	Inflation Rate (%)
Argentina	735.1	17,900	7.20	25.3
Australia	961	42,000	5.2	1.8
Brazil	2,330	11,700	5.5	5.4
Canada	1,474	42,300	7.3	1.5
China	12,260	9,100	6.5	2.6
France	2,238	35,300	9.8	2.2
Germany	3,167	38,700	5.5	2.1
India	4,716	3,800	8.5	9.7
Israel	260.9	33,900	6.9	1.7
Japan	4,576	35,900	4.4	0.0
Mexico	1,798	15,400	5.0	4.1
Russia	2,486	17,500	5.50	5.1
South Africa	576.1	11,300	25.1	5.7
United Kingdom	2,313	36,600	8.0	2.8
United States	16,803	51,700	7.4	2.1

Source: U.S. Department of Commerce Bureau of Economic Analysis, "National Economic Accounts"; The CIA, The World Fact Book.

TABLE 1.3
How Do We Evaluate Our Nation's Economy?

Unit of Measure	Description
Trade balance	The difference between our exports and our imports. If the balance is negative, as it has been since the mid-1980s, it is called a trade deficit and is generally viewed as unhealthy for our economy.
Consumer Price Index	Measures changes in prices of goods and services purchased for consumption by typical urban households.
Per capita income	Indicates the income level of "average" Americans. Useful in determining how much "average" consumers spend and how much money Americans are earning.
Unemployment rate	Indicates how many working-age Americans are not working who otherwise want to work.*
Inflation	Monitors price increases in consumer goods and services over specified periods of time. Used to determine if costs of goods and services are exceeding worker compensation over time.
Worker productivity	The amount of goods and services produced for each hour worked.

**Americans who do not work in a traditional sense, such as househusbands/housewives, are not counted as unemployed.*

Another important indicator of a nation's economic health is the relationship between its spending and income (from taxes). When a nation spends more than it takes in from taxes, it has a **budget deficit.** In the 1990s, the U.S. government eliminated its long-standing budget deficit by balancing the money spent for social, defense, and other programs with the amount of money taken in from taxes.

预算赤字
budget deficit
the condition in which a nation spends more than it takes in from taxes

In recent years, however, the budget deficit has reemerged and grown to record levels, partly due to defense spending in the aftermath of the terrorist attacks of September 11, 2001. Massive government stimulus spending during the most recent recession also increased the national debt. Because many Americans do not want their taxes increased and Congress has difficulty agreeing on appropriate tax rates, it is difficult to increase taxes and reduce the deficit. Like consumers and businesses, when the government needs money, it borrows from the public, banks, and even foreign investors. In 2013, the national debt (the amount of money the nation owes its lenders) exceeded $16 trillion, a new high.[17] This figure is especially worrisome because, to reduce the debt to a manageable level, the government either has to increase its revenues (raise taxes) or reduce spending on social, defense, and legal programs, neither of which is politically popular. The size of the national debt and little agreement on how to reduce the deficit caused the credit rating of the U.S. debt to go down in 2011. The national debt figure changes daily and can be seen at the Department of the Treasury, Bureau of the Public Debt, website. Table 1.3 describes some of the other ways we evaluate our nation's economy.

美国经济
The American Economy

LO 1-6

As we said previously, the United States is a mixed economy with a foundation based on capitalism. The answers to the three basic economic issues are determined primarily by competition and the forces of supply and demand, although the federal government does intervene in economic decisions to a certain extent. To understand the current state of the American economy and its effect on business practices, it is helpful to examine its history and the roles of the entrepreneur and the government.

Going Green

Luxury Automakers Embracing Eco-Friendly Interiors

What type of car uses bamboo, eucalyptus, reclaimed logs, or old fence posts in its interior? The answer is luxury cars. Consumers of luxury cars prefer natural wood interiors rather than plastic or fiberglass. While exotic wood increases the luxury of the vehicle, the most valuable wood comes from old-growth forests and other vulnerable areas. Instead, automakers are turning to wood from reclaimed logs and bamboo. Using these woods allows luxury car makers to differentiate themselves from competitors and appeal to the eco-conscious consumer.

Electric vehicle company Fisker has incorporated three types of reclaimed wood into its Karma sedans, including wood collected from areas damaged by forest fires, wood fallen to the bottom of lakes, and wood that fell during storms. BMW announced that its electric vehicle, the i3 plug-in, will have a eucalyptus interior, a plant that grows back quickly. Ford is using the tropical kenaf plant to replace oil-based materials in its Ford Escape. With more consumers desiring sustainable products, using plant-based materials can increase perceptions of brand value.

There might also be another reason for using plant-based materials in car construction. In addition to being more sustainable, some of these materials are lighter than traditional materials. For instance, Ford states that using kenaf plants to replace oil-based resins inside its doors reduces door bolsters by 25 percent. Lighter cars are more fuel-efficient, which saves consumers money on gasoline.[18]

Discussion Questions

1. Why might eco-friendly wood interior appeal to luxury car buyers?
2. What impact could using these plant-based materials have on the reputations of luxury automakers?
3. What are some benefits in using plant-based materials besides appealing to the luxury car buyer?

美国经济简史
A Brief History of the American Economy

早期的经济

The Early Economy. Before the colonization of North America, Native Americans lived as hunter/gatherers and farmers, with some trade among tribes. The colonists who came later operated primarily as an *agricultural economy*. People were self-sufficient and produced everything they needed at home, including food, clothing, and furniture. Abundant natural resources and a moderate climate nourished industries such as farming, fishing, shipping, and fur trading. A few manufactured goods and money for the colonies' burgeoning industries came from England and other countries.

As the nation expanded slowly toward the West, people found natural resources such as coal, copper, and iron ore and used them to produce goods such as horseshoes, farm implements, and kitchen utensils. Farm families who produced surplus goods sold or traded them for things they could not produce themselves, such as fine furniture and window glass. Some families also spent time turning raw materials into clothes and household goods. Because these goods were produced at home, this system was called the domestic system.

工业革命

The Industrial Revolution. The 19th century and the Industrial Revolution brought the development of new technology and factories. The factory brought together all the resources needed to make a product—materials, machines, and workers. Work in factories became specialized as workers focused on one or two tasks. As work became more efficient, productivity increased, making more goods available at lower prices. Railroads brought major changes, allowing farmers to send their surplus crops and goods all over the nation for barter or for sale.

Factories began to spring up along the railways to manufacture farm equipment and a variety of other goods to be shipped by rail. Samuel Slater set up the first

American textile factory after he memorized the plans for an English factory and emigrated to the United States. Eli Whitney revolutionized the cotton industry with his cotton gin. Francis Cabot Lowell's factory organized all the steps in manufacturing cotton cloth for maximum efficiency and productivity. John Deere's farm equipment increased farm production and reduced the number of farmers required to feed the young nation. Farmers began to move to cities to find jobs in factories and a higher standard of living. Henry Ford developed the assembly-line system to produce automobiles. Workers focused on one part of an automobile and then pushed it to the next stage until it rolled off the assembly line as a finished automobile. Ford's assembly line could manufacture many automobiles efficiently, and the price of his cars was $200, making them affordable to many Americans.

制造业经济和市场经济

The Manufacturing and Marketing Economies. Industrialization brought increased prosperity, and the United States gradually became a *manufacturing economy*—one devoted to manufacturing goods and providing services rather than producing agricultural products. The assembly line was applied to more industries, increasing the variety of goods available to the consumer. Businesses became more concerned with the needs of the consumer and entered the *marketing economy*. Expensive goods such as cars and appliances could be purchased on a time-payment plan. Companies conducted research to find out what products consumers needed and wanted. Advertising made consumers aware of products and important information about features, prices, and other competitive advantages.

Because these developments occurred in a free-enterprise system, consumers determined what goods and services were produced. They did this by purchasing the products they liked at prices they were willing to pay. The United States prospered, and American citizens had one of the highest standards of living in the world.

服务业和数字经济

The Service and New Digital Economy. After World War II, with the increased standard of living, Americans had more money and more time. They began to pay others to perform services that made their lives easier. Beginning in the 1960s, more and more women entered the workforce. The United States began experiencing major shifts in the population. The U.S. population grew 9.7 percent in the past decade to about 316 million. This is the slowest pace of growth since the Great Depression, with the South leading the population gains. While the birth rate in the United States is declining, new immigrants help with population gains.[19] The profile of the family is also changing: Today there are more single parent families and individuals living alone, and in two parent families, both parents often work.

One result of this trend is that time-pressed Americans are increasingly paying others to do tasks they used to do at home, like cooking, laundry, landscaping, and child care. These trends have gradually changed the United States to a *service economy*—one devoted to the production of services that make life easier for busy consumers. Businesses increased their demand for services, especially in the areas of finance and information technology. Service industries such as restaurants, banking, health care, child care, auto repair, leisure-related industries, and even education are growing rapidly and may account for as much as 80 percent of the U.S. economy. These trends continue with advanced technology contributing to new service products based on technology and digital media that provide smart phones, social networking, and virtual worlds. Table 1.4 provides evidence that the new digital economy is changing how we use information and the service industry.

DID YOU KNOW? **Approximately 59 percent of adult women are engaged in the workforce.**[20]

TABLE 1.4
Cell Phone Activities

The % of cell phone owners who use their cell phone to . . .	
81	send or receive text messages
60	access the Internet
52	send or receive email
50	download apps
49	get directions, recommendations, or other location-based information
48	listen to music
21	participate in a video call or video chat
8	"check in" or share your location

Source: Pew Research Center's Internet & American Life Project Spring Tracking Survey, April 17–May 19, 2013. N = 2,076 cell phone owners. Interviews were conducted in English and Spanish and on landline and cell phones. The margin of error for results based on all cell phone owners is +/− 2.4 percentage points.

企业家的作用
The Role of the Entrepreneur

企业家
entrepreneur
an individual who risks his or her wealth, time, and effort to develop for profit an innovative product or way of doing something

An **entrepreneur** is an individual who risks his or her wealth, time, and effort to develop for profit an innovative product or way of doing something. Nick Woodman is a true American entrepreneur. At 26, Woodman—who was an avid surfer—identified the need to film events from the athlete's perspective. He developed GoPro Inc., which makes wearable cameras that are easily attachable to surfboards, ski helmets, and other equipment. Consumers who used a GoPro camera inundated YouTube with their own amateur videos, leading to strong word-of-mouth marketing. GoPro became so popular that Woodman and the company's backers want to take the firm public—at a valuation of more than $2.3 billion.[21]

The free-enterprise system provides the conditions necessary for entrepreneurs to succeed. In the past, entrepreneurs were often inventors who brought all the factors of production together to produce a new product. Thomas Edison, whose inventions include the record player and lightbulb, was an early American entrepreneur. Henry Ford was one of the first persons to develop mass assembly methods in the automobile industry. Other entrepreneurs, so-called captains of industry, invested in the country's growth. John D. Rockefeller built Standard Oil out of the fledgling oil industry, and Andrew Carnegie invested in railroads and founded the United States Steel Corporation. Andrew Mellon built the Aluminum Company of America and Gulf Oil. J.P. Morgan started financial institutions to fund the business activities of other entrepreneurs. Although these entrepreneurs were born in another century, their legacy to the American economy lives on in the companies they started, many of which still operate today. Colonel Eli Lilly in Indianapolis, Indiana, was continually frustrated with the quality of pharmaceutical products sold at the time. As a pharmaceutical chemist, he decided to start his own firm that would offer the highest-quality medicines. His firm, Eli Lilly and Company, would go on to make landmark achievements, including being one of the first pharmaceutical firms to mass-produce penicillin. Today, Eli Lilly is the 10th largest pharmaceutical firm in the world.[22]

Entrepreneurs are constantly changing American business practices with new technology and innovative management techniques. Bill Gates, for example, built

Entrepreneurship in Action

Emeco Makes Indestructible Chairs

Electric Machine and Equipment Company (Emeco)
Founder: Wilton Carlyle Dinges
Founded: 1944, in Hanover, Pennsylannia
Success: Although it started out with the Navy as its only customer, Emeco's chair products are now common in businesses across the world.

Emeco was founded to make chairs for the Navy during World War II. The chairs had to meet certain specifications, such as the ability to withstand water, salt air, and sailors. The result was the virtually indestructible 1006, or the Navy Chair. It was made from aluminum and underwent a proprietary 77-step handmade process still used today.

After the war, however, Emeco faced difficulties. The indestructible nature of the chairs reduced the need for replacement orders. Then Emeco discovered that a designer named Philippe Starck was incorporating the chairs into his redesign of New York's Paramount Hotel. Emeco partnered with Starck to create redesigns that would appeal to more customers. This marked the beginning of a new personality for Emeco.

Over the years, Emeco has increased its clientele. Its chairs are commonly found in restaurants and airports and are even featured in movies. Coca-Cola has approached Emeco to create a version of the 1006 chair made from 111 recycled plastic bottles. Business markets appreciate the chairs' ability to withstand extreme pressure, while others enjoy the beautiful designs suitable for art gallery exhibits. Collaborating with designers has allowed Emeco to continue for more than 70 years.[23]

Microsoft, a software company whose products include Word and Windows, into a multibillion-dollar enterprise. Frederick Smith had an idea to deliver packages overnight, and now his FedEx Company plays an important role in getting documents and packages delivered all over the world for businesses and individuals. Steve Jobs co-founded Apple and turned the company into a successful consumer electronics firm that revolutionized many different industries, with products such as the iPod, iPhone, Mac computers, and iPad. The company went from near bankruptcy in the 1990s to become one of the most valuable brands in the entire world. Entrepreneurs have been associated with such uniquely American concepts as Dell Computers, Ben & Jerry's, Levi's, McDonald's, Dr Pepper, Apple, Google, Facebook, and Walmart. Walmart, founded by entrepreneur Sam Walton, was the first retailer to reach $100 billion in sales in one year and now routinely passes that mark, with more than $466 billion in 2013.[24]

Google Wallet is a mobile payments system that allows users to store their credit card or debit card information. When checking out at stores, users can bring up the app and use the information to pay for their purchases.

政府在美国经济中的作用
The Role of Government in the American Economy

The American economic system is best described as modified capitalism because the government regulates business to preserve competition and protect consumers and employees. Federal, state, and local governments intervene in the economy with laws and regulations designed to promote competition and to protect consumers, employees, and the environment. Many of these laws are discussed in Appendix B.

Additionally, government agencies such as the U.S. Department of Commerce measure the health of the economy (GDP, productivity, etc.) and, when necessary, take steps to minimize the disruptive effects of

Many companies engage in socially responsible behavior to give back to their communities. Home Depot partners with Habitat for Humanity to build homes for disadvantaged families.

economic fluctuations and reduce unemployment. When the economy is contracting and unemployment is rising, the federal government through the Federal Reserve Board tries to spur growth so that consumers will spend more money and businesses will hire more employees. To accomplish this, it may reduce interest rates or increase its own spending for goods and services. When the economy expands so fast that infl ation results, the government may intervene to reduce infl ation by slowing down economic growth. This can be accomplished by raising interest rates to discourage spending by businesses and consumers.

商业伦理与社会责任在企业中的作用
The Role of Ethics and Social Responsibility in Business

In the past few years, you may have read about a number of scandals at a number of well-known corporations, including Enron, Countrywide Financial, BP, and even leading banks such as Bank of America and Citigroup. In many cases, misconduct by individuals within these firms had an adverse effect on current and retired employees, investors, and others associated with these firms. In some cases, individuals went to jail for their actions. Top executives like Enron's Jeffrey Skilling and Tyco's Dennis Kozlowski received long prison sentences for their roles in corporate misconduct. These scandals undermined public confidence in corporate America and sparked a new debate about ethics in business. Business ethics generally refers to the standards and principles used by society to define appropriate and inappropriate conduct in the workplace. In many cases, these standards have been codified as laws prohibiting actions deemed unacceptable.

Society is increasingly demanding that businesspeople behave ethically and socially responsibly toward not only their customers but also employees, investors, government regulators, communities, and the natural environment. No area is more debated as online piracy. Software, music, and film executives want to defend their intellectual property. On the other hand, companies such as Google are concerned that strict laws would stifle innovation and enable censorship.[25] When actions are heavily criticized, a balance is usually required to support and protect various stakeholders.

While one view is that ethics and social responsibility are a good supplement to business activities, there is an alternative viewpoint. Research has shown that ethical behavior can not only enhance a company's reputation but can also drive profits.[26] The ethical and socially responsible conduct of companies such as Whole Foods, Starbucks, and the hotel chain Marriott provides evidence that good ethics is good business. There is growing recognition that the long-term value of conducting business in an ethical and socially responsible manner that considers the interests of all stakeholders creates superior financial performance.[27]

To promote socially responsible and ethical behavior while achieving organizational goals, businesses can monitor changes and trends in society's values. Businesses should determine what society wants and attempt to predict the long-term effects of their decisions. While it requires an effort to address the interests of all stakeholders, businesses can prioritize and attempt to balance conflicting demands. The goal is to develop a solid reputation of trust and avoid misconduct to develop effective workplace ethics.

在课堂上学习商业知识，可能吗
Can You Learn Business in a Classroom?

Obviously, the answer is yes, or there would be no purpose for this textbook! To be successful in business, you need knowledge, skills, experience, and good judgment. The topics covered in this chapter and throughout this book provide some of the knowledge you need to understand the world of business. The opening vignette at the beginning of each chapter, boxes, examples within each chapter, and the case at the end of each chapter describe experiences to help you develop good business judgment. The "Build Your Skills" exercise at the end of each chapter and the "Solve the Dilemma" box will help you develop skills that may be useful in your future career. However, good judgment is based on knowledge and experience plus personal insight and understanding. Therefore, you need more courses in business, along with some practical experience in the business world, to help you develop the special insight necessary to put your personal stamp on knowledge as you apply it. The challenge in business is in the area of judgment, and judgment does not develop from memorizing an introductory business textbook. If you are observant in your daily experiences as an employee, as a student, and as a consumer, you will improve your ability to make good business judgments.

So You Want a Job in the Business World

When most people think of a career in business, they see themselves entering the door to large companies and multinationals that they read about in the news and that are discussed in class. In a national survey, students indicated they would like to work for Google, Walt Disney, Apple, and Ernst & Young. In fact, most jobs are not with large corporations, but are in small companies, nonprofit organizations, government, and even self-employed individuals. There are nearly 22 million individuals who own their own businesses and have no employees. With more than 75 percent of the economy based on services, there are jobs available in industries, such as health care, finance, education, hospitality, entertainment, and transportation. The world is changing quickly and large corporations replace the equivalent of their entire workforce every four years.

The fast pace of technology today means that you have to be prepared to take advantage of emerging job opportunities and markets. You must also become adaptive and recognize that business is becoming more global, with job opportunities around the world. If you want to obtain such a job, you shouldn't miss a chance to spend some time overseas. To get you started on the path to thinking about job opportunities, consider all of the changes in business today that might affect your possible long-term track and that could bring you lots of success. You may want to stay completely out of large organizations and corporations and put yourself in a position for an entrepreneurial role as a self-employed contractor or small-business owner. However, there are many who feel that experience in larger businesses is helpful to your success later as an entrepreneur.

You're on the road to learning the key knowledge, skills, and trends that you can use to be a star in business. Business's impact on our society, especially in the area of sustainability and improvement of the environment, is a growing challenge and opportunity. Green businesses and green jobs in the business world are provided to give you a glimpse at the possibilities. Along the way, we will introduce you to some specific careers and offer advice on developing your own job opportunities. Research indicates that you won't be that happy with your job unless you enjoy your work and feel that it has a purpose. Since you spend most of your waking hours every day at work, you need to seriously think about what is important to you in a job.[28]

Review Your Understanding

Define basic concepts such as business, product, and profit.

A business is an organization or individual that seeks a profit by providing products that satisfy people's needs. A product is a good, service, or idea that has both tangible and intangible characteristics that provide satisfaction and benefits. Profit, the basic goal of business, is the difference between what it costs to make and sell a product and what a customer pays for it.

Identify the main participants and activities of business and explain why studying business is important.

The three main participants in business are owners, employees, and customers, but others—government regulators, suppliers, social groups, etc.—are also important. Management involves planning, organizing, and controlling the tasks required to carry out the work of the company. Marketing refers to those activities—research, product development, promotion, pricing, and distribution—designed to provide goods and services that satisfy customers. Finance refers to activities concerned with funding a business and using its funds effectively. Studying business can help you prepare for a career and become a better consumer.

Define economics and compare the four types of economic systems.

Economics is the study of how resources are distributed for the production of goods and services within a social system; an economic system describes how a particular society distributes its resources. Communism is an economic system in which the people, without regard to class, own all the nation's resources. In a socialist system, the government owns and operates basic industries, but individuals own most businesses. Under capitalism, individuals own and operate the majority of businesses that provide goods and services. Mixed economies have elements from more than one economic system; most countries have mixed economies.

Describe the role of supply, demand, and competition in a free-enterprise system.

In a free-enterprise system, individuals own and operate the majority of businesses, and the distribution of resources is determined by competition, supply, and demand. Demand is the number of goods and services that consumers are willing to buy at different prices at a specific time. Supply is the number of goods or services that businesses are willing to sell at different prices at a specific time. The price at which the supply of a product equals demand at a specific point in time is the equilibrium price. Competition is the rivalry among businesses to convince consumers to buy goods or services. Four types of competitive environments are pure competition, monopolistic competition, oligopoly, and monopoly. These economic concepts determine how businesses may operate in a particular society and, often, how much they can charge for their products.

Specify why and how the health of the economy is measured.

A country measures the state of its economy to determine whether it is expanding or contracting and whether the country needs to take steps to minimize fluctuations. One commonly used measure is gross domestic product (GDP), the sum of all goods and services produced in a country during a year. A budget deficit occurs when a nation spends more than it takes in from taxes.

Trace the evolution of the American economy and discuss the role of the entrepreneur in the economy.

The American economy has evolved through several stages: the early economy, the Industrial Revolution, the manufacturing economy, the marketing economy, and the service and Internet-based economy of today. Entrepreneurs play an important role because they risk their time, wealth, and efforts to develop new goods, services, and ideas that fuel the growth of the American economy.

Evaluate a small-business owner's situation and propose a course of action.

"Solve the Dilemma" on page 29 presents a problem for the owner of the firm. Should you, as the owner, raise prices, expand operations, or form a venture with a larger company to deal with demand? You should be able to apply your newfound understanding of the relationship between supply and demand to assess the situation and reach a decision about how to proceed.

Revisit the World of Business

Revisit the World of Business Questions

- Why is competition important in a capitalist economy?
- Why do businesses need to focus on both primary competitors and newer entrants?
- How was Red Bull able to become a major competitor in an industry dominated by two main players?

Learn the Terms

budget deficit
business
capitalism (free enterprise)
communism
competition
demand
depression
economic contraction
economic expansion
economic system
economics
entrepreneur
equilibrium price
financial resources
free-market system
gross domestic product (GDP)
human resources
inflation
mixed economies
monopolistic competition
monopoly
natural resources
nonprofit organizations
oligopoly
product
profit
pure competition
recession
socialism
stakeholders
supply
unemployment

Check Your Progress

1. What is the fundamental goal of business? Do all organizations share this goal?
2. Name the forms a product may take and give some examples of each.
3. Who are the main participants of business? What are the main activities? What other factors have an impact on the conduct of business in the United States?
4. What are four types of economic systems? Can you provide an example of a country using each type?

5. Explain the terms *supply, demand, equilibrium price,* and *competition.* How do these forces interact in the American economy?
6. List the four types of competitive environments and provide an example of a product of each environment.
7. List and define the various measures governments may use to gauge the state of their economies. If unemployment is high, will the growth of GDP be great or small?
8. Why are fluctuations in the economy harmful?
9. How did the Industrial Revolution influence the growth of the American economy? Why do we apply the term *service economy* to the United States today?
10. Explain the federal government's role in the American economy.

Get Involved

1. Discuss the economic changes occurring in Russia and eastern European countries, which once operated as communist economic systems. Why are these changes occurring? What do you think the result will be?
2. Why is it important for the government to measure the economy? What kinds of actions might it take to control the economy's growth?
3. Is the American economy currently expanding or contracting? Defend your answer with the latest statistics on GDP, inflation, unemployment, and so on. How is the federal government responding?

Build Your Skills

The Forces of Supply and Demand

Background

WagWumps are a new children's toy with the potential to be a highly successful product. WagWumps are cute and furry, and their eyes glow in the dark. Each family set consists of a mother, a father, and two children. Wee-Toys' manufacturing costs are about $6 per set, with $3 representing marketing and distribution costs. The wholesale price of a WagWump family for a retailer is $15.75, and the toy carries a suggested retail price of $26.99.

Task

Assume you are a decision maker at a retailer, such as Target or Walmart, that must determine the price the stores in your district

FIGURE 1.5
Equilibrium Price of WagWumps

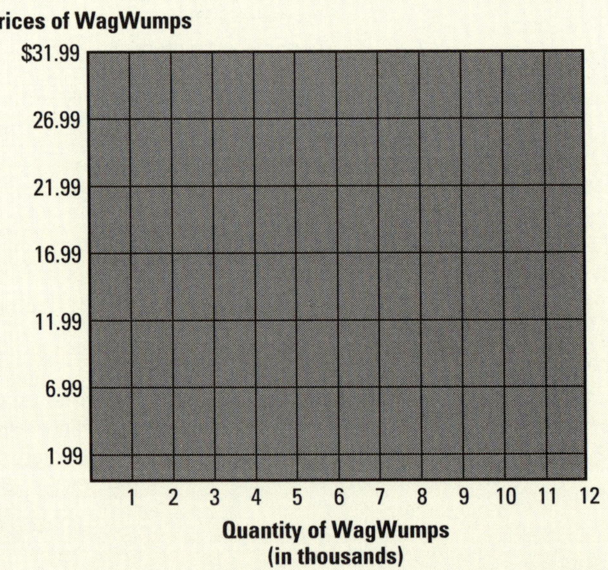

should charge customers for the WagWump family set. From the information provided, you know that the SRP (suggested retail price) is $26.99 per set and that your company can purchase the toy set from your wholesaler for $15.75 each. Based on the following assumptions, plot your company's supply curve on the graph provided in Figure 1.5 and label it "supply curve."

Quantity	Price
3,000	$16.99
5,000	21.99
7,000	26.99

Using the following assumptions, plot your customers' demand curve on Figure 1.5 and label it "demand curve."

Quantity	Price
10,000	$16.99
6,000	21.99
2,000	26.99

For this specific time, determine the point at which the quantity of toys your company is willing to supply equals the quantity of toys the customers in your sales district are willing to buy and label that point "equilibrium price."

Solve the Dilemma

Mrs. Acres Homemade Pies

Shelly Acres, whose grandmother gave her a family recipe for making pies, loved to cook, and she decided to start a business she called Mrs. Acres Homemade Pies. The company produces specialty pies and sells them in local supermarkets and select family restaurants. In each of the first six months, Shelly and three part-time employees sold 2,000 pies for $4.50 each, netting $1.50 profit per pie. The pies were quite successful and Shelly could not keep up with demand. The company's success results from a quality product and productive employees who are motivated by incentives and who enjoy being part of a successful new business.

To meet demand, Shelly expanded operations, borrowing money and increasing staff to four full-time employees. Production and sales increased to 8,000 pies per month, and profits soared to $12,000 per month. However, demand for Mrs. Acres Homemade Pies continues to accelerate beyond what Shelly can supply. She has several options: (1) maintain current production levels and raise prices; (2) expand the facility and staff while maintaining the current price; or (3) contract the production of the pies to a national restaurant chain, giving Shelly a percentage of profits with minimal involvement.

Discussion Questions

1. Explain and demonstrate the relationship between supply and demand for Mrs. Acres Homemade Pies.
2. What challenges does Shelly face as she considers the three options?
3. What would you do in Shelly's position?

Build Your Business Plan

The Dynamics of Business and Economics

Have you ever thought about owning your business? If you have, how did your idea come about? Is it your experience with this particular field? Or might it be an idea that evolved from your desires for a particular good or service not being offered in your community? For example, perhaps you and your friends have yearned for a place to go have coffee, relax, and talk. Now is an opportunity to create the café bar you have been thinking of!

Whether you consider yourself a visionary or a practical thinker, think about your community. What needs are not being met? While it is tempting to suggest a new restaurant (maybe even one near campus), easier-to-implement business plans can range from a lawn care business or a designated driver business to a placement service agency for teenagers.

Once you have an idea for a business plan, think about how profitable this idea might be. Is there sufficient demand for this business? How large is the market for this particular business? What about competitors? How many are there?

To learn about your industry, you should do a thorough search of your initial ideas of a product on the Internet.

See for Yourself Videocase

Redbox Succeeds by Identifying Market Need

Redbox's tell-tale bright red kiosks in stores and fast-food restaurants across the country have become an image of what a great business model can accomplish. The company's ability to offer customers a convenient and inexpensive DVD rental option has allowed them to grow despite the widespread growth of streaming services such as Netflix and Amazon. In addition, Redbox has responded competitively by partnering with Verizon to offer their own streaming service in conjunction with DVD rentals. As one of the top rental companies in the United States, Redbox is a true entrepreneurial success story.

Building Redbox into a successful firm was not easy, however. It was fraught with challenges. Like most successful companies, Redbox started out by identifying a need. It recognized that consumers could not often find the movies they wanted in convenient locations. Like all good ideas, Redbox required funding to get started. This proved to be a major difficulty. Realizing that customers did not want to pay much for renting movies, Redbox decided to charge only one dollar. Yet the kiosks, which contain over 800 components, required a large amount of capital. The combination of the capital-intensive nature of the business and the low prices was not an attractive recipe for venture capital funding.

However, Redbox was certain that demand for its product offerings would exceed the costs. The company finally found a partner in the more established Outerwall, formerly known as Coinstar, which already had partnerships with many different retailers. The alliance opened the way for Redbox to begin installing kiosks at the front of stores.

Redbox did not immediately expand across the country. Instead, it took a cautious approach toward its business model. It began by focusing its efforts on making one kiosk profitable, then replicating this way of thinking regionally and nationally. In this way, Redbox was able to test its concept without taking the risk of widespread failure.

Even though it was expanding, it was some time before Redbox was able to earn a profit. Like all entrepreneurs, the founders of Redbox had to take many risks if they wanted the company to succeed. "The risks for starting Redbox were significant," said Marc Achler, vice president of new business, strategy, and innovation. "The first couple years we had some red ink. It took us a while before we turned profitable." Yet with persistence and continual relationship building with retailers, Redbox has been able to secure more than 50 percent of the DVD-rental market.

One way that Redbox has been able to secure such a large share of the market is by meeting the needs of a variety of stakeholders. Redbox views its customers as its first priority and has developed its kiosks and database to meet their needs. For instance, customers can reserve movies online and pick them up at their nearest kiosk. If a kiosk happens to be out of a particular movie, customers can search the Redbox database to locate the movie at a nearby kiosk. This combination of convenience and low prices has attracted customers who desire a simplified process to renting movies. The same is true for their streaming service, Redbox Instant by Verizon, which offers unlimited streaming for the same price as competitors and the option to purchase DVDs from the site.

Additionally, Redbox has created a process that also benefits the needs of its retail partners. Redbox kiosks help attract consumers to the store, where they may purchase additional products. Customers must come back the next day to return their movie, where they may once again purchase more products from the retailer. In this way, Redbox creates a win-win situation for both itself and its partners.

This is not to say that everything is easy for Redbox. For instance, it must continually safeguard against allowing underage children to rent inappropriate (rated-R) movies. And while Redbox has approached this changing and dynamic marketplace proactively, it must continue to do so in order to maintain its competitive position. The company's ability to price rentals and streaming services at 70 percent of the price of competitors and still make a 6 percent return is impressive, but this can easily change as competitors find ways to lower their prices or consumers' desires change.[33]

Discussion Questions

1. Why are consumers so willing to rent from Redbox?
2. How was Redbox able to overcome some of its earliest challenges?
3. What are some recommendations for ways that Redbox can maintain its high market share?

You can find the related video in the Video Library in Connect. Ask your instructor how you can access Connect.

Team Exercise

Major economic systems, including capitalism, socialism, and communism, as well as mixed economies, were discussed in this chapter. Assuming that you want an economic system that is best for the majority, not just a few members of society, defend one of the economic systems as the best system. Form groups and try to reach agreement on one economic system. Defend why you support the system that you advance.

附录 A

商业计划撰写指南
Guidelines for the Development of the Business Plan

These guidelines are for students to create a hypothetical business plan for a good/service/business of their choice. Students should assume to have $25,000 to start this new business in their community.

At the end of every chapter, there will be a section entitled "Build Your Business Plan" to assist you in the development of the business plan.

第一阶段：商业计划的制定
Phase 1: Development of the Business Proposal

You are encouraged to submit your idea for approval to your instructor as soon as possible. This will eliminate wasted effort on an idea that is not feasible in the instructor's view. Business plan proposals will be evaluated based on their thoroughness and your ability to provide support for the idea.

The business proposal consists of the following elements.

业务描述

Business Description. This consists of an overview of the existing good/service or the good/service/business you will be starting (manufacturer, merchandiser, or service provider). This includes developing a mission (reason for existence; overall purpose of the firm) and a rationale for why you believe this business will be a success. What is your vision for this proposed product/business?

简要的营销计划

Brief Marketing Plan. (The marketing plan will be further developed as the plan evolves.) A description of your business/product is required. Identify the target market and develop a strategy for appealing to it. Justify your proposed location for this business. Describe how you will promote the new business and provide a rationale for your pricing strategy. Select a name for this business. The name should be catchy yet relate to the competencies of the business.

竞争分析

Competitive Analysis. Identify the competition as broadly as possible. Indicate why this business will be successful given the market.

第二阶段：最终的书面商业计划
Phase 2: Final Written Business Plan

执行摘要

Executive Summary. The executive summary appears first but should be written last.

企业描述

Business Description. This section requires fleshing out the body of the business plan, including material from your revised preliminary proposal with more data, charts, and appendices. Include a description of the proposed form of organization, either a partnership or corporation, and the rationalization of the form chosen.

行业与市场分析

Industry and Market Analysis. An analysis of the industry including the growth rate of the industry and number of new entrants into this field is necessary. Identify uncontrollable variables within the industry. Determine an estimate of the proposed realistic size of the potential market. This will require interpretation of statistics from the U.S. census as well as from local sources such as the Chamber of Commerce.

竞争分析

Competitive Analysis. Include an exhaustive list of the primary and secondary competition, along with the competitive advantage of each.

营销策略

Marketing Strategy. Target market specifics need to be developed.

Decisions on the marketing mix variables need to be made:

- Price (at the market, below market, above market)
- Promotion (sales associates, advertising budget, use of sales promotions, and publicity/goodwill)
- Distribution—Rationale of choice and level of distribution
- Product/Service—A detailed rationale of the perceived differential advantage of your product offering

运营问题

Operational Issues. How will you make or provide your product? Location rationale, facility type, leasing considerations, and sources of suppliers need to be detailed. Software/hardware requirements necessary to maintain operations must be determined.

人力资源需求

Human Resources Requirement. Number and description of personnel needed, including realistic required education and skills.

财务预测

Financial Projections. Statement of cash flows must be prepared for the first 12 months of the business. This must include startup costs, opening expenses, and estimation of cash inflows and outflows. A breakeven analysis should be included and an explanation of your expected financial expenditures.

附录部分

Appendixes

第三阶段：口头报告
Phase 3: Oral Presentation

Specific separate guidelines on the oral presentation will be provided.

2 Business Ethics and Social Responsibility

商业伦理与社会责任

Learning Objectives

After reading this chapter, you will be able to:

LO 2-1 Define business ethics and social responsibility and examine their importance.

LO 2-2 Detect some of the ethical issues that may arise in business.

LO 2-3 Specify how businesses can promote ethical behavior.

LO 2-4 Explain the four dimensions of social responsibility.

LO 2-5 Debate an organization's social responsibilities to owners, employees, consumers, the environment, and the community.

LO 2-6 Evaluate the ethics of a business's decision.

Chapter Outline

进入商业世界

Enter the World of Business

抗菌肥皂面临监管部门和消费者的双重压力

Antibacterial Soap Faces Regulatory and Consumer Pressure

The soap industry is a strong business within the United States, amounting to more than $5 billion in sales of soaps, shower products, and body washes. However, the industry has come under scrutiny over product safety and validity of claims, which could lead to significant decreases in profits. If the soap is used too often, a chemical called triclosan—found in approximately 75 percent of antibacterial products—could lead to bacteria that are not only resistant to triclosan but to other antibiotics as well. Consumer advocates are also concerned that triclosan might interfere with hormones, making long-term use harmful for the body. In addition, critics claim that triclosan is not any more effective than regular soap and water. Studies have revealed the presence of triclosan in urine samples of 75 percent of respondents, suggesting that this chemical is highly present among the general population.

The Food and Drug Administration (FDA) has proposed that antibacterial soap and body wash manufacturers provide additional evidence that their products are more effective than comparable products and are safe for long-term use. If the proposal of the FDA goes through, it will have significant implications for soap manufacturers and other industries, such as cosmetics, that use triclosan in their products. If antibacterial soap manufacturers cannot prove their claims of effectiveness, they might have to relabel their products, reformulate them, or even remove them completely, which would be costly. Increased concern is causing some firms to begin to voluntarily remove triclosan. Johnson and Johnson and Reckitt Benckiser have begun phasing out triclosan from many of their products.[1]

引言
Introduction

Any organization, including nonprofits, has to manage the ethical behavior of employees and participants in the overall operations of the organization. Misconduct can take on many forms within the business environment, including deceptive business practices and the withholding of important information from investors or consumers. Wrongdoing by some businesses has focused public attention and government involvement on encouraging more acceptable business conduct. Any organizational decision may be judged as right or wrong, ethical or unethical, legal or illegal.

In this chapter, we take a look at the role of ethics and social responsibility in business decision making. First we define business ethics and examine why it is important to understand ethics' role in business. Next we explore a number of business ethics issues to help you learn to recognize such issues when they arise. Finally, we consider steps businesses can take to improve ethical behavior in their organizations. The second half of the chapter focuses on social responsibility and unemployment. We survey some important issues and detail how companies have responded to them.

商业伦理与社会责任
Business Ethics and Social Responsibility

LO 2-1

商业伦理
business ethics
principles and standards that determine acceptable conduct in business

In this chapter, we define **business ethics** as the principles and standards that determine acceptable conduct in business organizations. Personal ethics, on the other hand, relates to an individual's values, principles, and standards of conduct. The acceptability of behavior in business is determined by not only the organization but also stakeholders such as customers, competitors, government regulators, interest groups, and the public, as well as each individual's personal principles and values. The publicity and debate surrounding highly visible legal and ethical issues at a number of well-known firms, including Diamond Foods, Target, and J.P. Morgan, highlight the need for businesses to integrate ethics and responsibility into all business decisions. For instance, Target was criticized for not having appropriate internal controls in place to prevent the theft of millions of their customers' credit and debit card accounts. Most unethical activities within organizations are supported by an organizational culture that encourages employees to bend the rules. On the other hand, trust in business is the glue that holds relationships together. In Figure 2.1, you can see that trust in banks is lower than in other industries, except for government.

Organizations that exhibit a high ethical culture encourage employees to act with integrity and adhere to business values. Many experts agree that ethical leadership, ethical values, and compliance are important in creating good business ethics. To truly create an ethical culture, however, managers must show a strong commitment to ethics and compliance. This "tone at the top" requires top managers to acknowledge their own role in supporting ethics and compliance, create strong relationships with the general counsel and the ethics and compliance department, clearly communicate company expectations for ethical behavior to all employees, educate all managers and supervisors in the business about the company's ethics policies, and train managers and employees on what to do if an ethics crisis occurs.[2]

社会责任
social responsibility
a business's obligation to maximize its positive impact and minimize its negative impact on society

Many consumers and social advocates believe that businesses should not only make a profit but also consider the social implications of their activities. We define **social responsibility** as a business's obligation to maximize its positive impact and minimize its negative impact on society. Although many people use the terms *social responsibility* and *ethics* interchangeably, they do not mean the same thing. Business ethics relates to an *individual's* or a *work group's* decisions that society evaluates as right or

Entrepreneurship in Action

Listening for a Good Business Opportunity

OrigAudio
Founders: Jason Lucash and Mike Szymczak
Founded: 2009, in Costa Mesa, California
Success: OrigAudio released a recyclable foldable speaker that has helped the firm double its sales every year since its founding.

Jason Lucash and Mike Szymczak got the idea for their company from a Chinese food takeout box! This simple item inspired them to start OrigAudio and launch their first product: a set of portable speakers made out of recycled materials that can fold up! These speakers are made with 70 percent post-recycled materials and require no external power sources. After being seen at a trade show by a QVC representative, the speakers were featured on the Home Shopping Network and sold more than $750,000 worth in two years. OrigAudio embraces simple products that make lives easier for consumers. For instance, it sells small devices that allow consumers to turn ordinary items into speakers. It also demonstrates social responsibility with its "Beet" product line. For every pair of Beets headphones it sells, OrigAudio donates a can of beets to the Second Harvest Food Bank of Orange County. To date, the company's recycled speakers and other items are sold on its website and in some well-known retail locations such as Bed, Bath, and Beyond.[3]

wrong, whereas social responsibility is a broader concept that concerns the impact of the *entire business's* activities on society. From an ethical perspective, for example, we may be concerned about a health care organization overcharging the government for Medicare services. From a social responsibility perspective, we might be concerned about the impact that this overcharging will have on the ability of the health care system to provide adequate services for all citizens. It would appear that such concern is warranted. In 2013, a Detroit-based oncologist was charged with purposefully misdiagnosing patients and then charging Medicaid for their treatment. Not only was this a serious case of health care fraud, it also endangered the safety of patients.[4]

The most basic ethical and social responsibility concerns have been codified by laws and regulations that encourage businesses to conform to society's standards, values, and attitudes. For example, after accounting scandals at a number of well-known firms in the

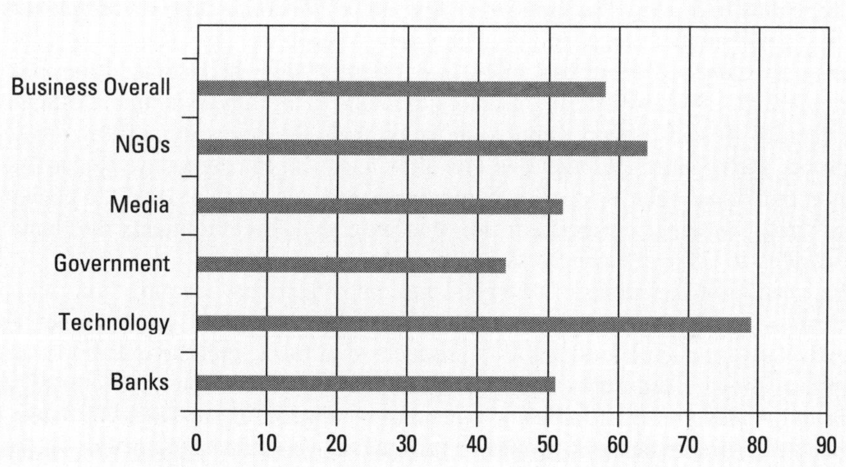

FIGURE 2.1
Global Trust in Different Institutions

Source: Edelman Trust Barometer: 2014 Annual Global Study.

TABLE 2.1 Timeline of Ethical and Socially Responsible Activities

1960s	1970s	1980s	1990s	2000s
• Social issues • Consumer Bill of Rights • Disadvantaged consumer • Environmental issues • Product safety	• Business ethics • Social responsibility • Diversity • Bribery • Discrimination • Identifying ethical issues	• Standards for ethical conduct • Financial misconduct • Self-regulation • Codes of conduct • Ethics training	• Corporate ethics programs • Regulation to support business ethics • Health issues • Safe working conditions • Detecting misconduct	• Transparency in financial markets • Corporate misconduct • Intellectual property • Regulation of accounting and finance • Executive compensation

Source: Adapted from "Business Ethics Timeline," copyright © 2003, Ethics Resource Center *(n.d.).*

early 2000s shook public confidence in the integrity of corporate America, the reputations of every U.S. company suffered regardless of their association with the scandals.[5] To help restore confidence in corporations and markets, Congress passed the Sarbanes-Oxley Act, which criminalized securities fraud and stiffened penalties for corporate fraud. After the financial crisis occurred in the most recent recession, the Dodd-Frank Act was passed to reform the financial industry and offer consumers protection against complex and/or deceptive financial products. At a minimum, managers are expected to obey all laws and regulations. Most legal issues arise as choices that society deems unethical, irresponsible, or otherwise unacceptable. However, all actions deemed unethical by society are not necessarily illegal, and both legal and ethical concerns change over time (see Table 2.1). Business law refers to the laws and regulations that govern the conduct of business. Many problems and conflicts in business can be avoided if owners, managers, and employees knew more about business law and the legal system. Business ethics, social responsibility, and laws together act as a compliance system, requiring that businesses and employees act responsibly in society. In this chapter, we explore ethics and social responsibility; Appendix B addresses business law, including the Sarbanes-Oxley Act and the Dodd-Frank Act.

伦理在企业中的作用
The Role of Ethics in Business

You have only to pick up *The Wall Street Journal* or *USA Today* to see examples of the growing concern about legal and ethical issues in business. For example, the federal government launched an investigation into whether Avon had violated the Foreign Corrupt Practices Act by offering gifts or payments to foreign government officials to gain licenses. Because Avon wants to move on from the crisis, it is offering to settle the probe. Such a large settlement will result in a loss for the company.[6] Regardless of what an individual believes about a particular action, if society judges it to be unethical or wrong, whether correctly or not, that judgment directly affects the organization's ability to achieve its business goals.[7]

Well-publicized incidents of unethical and illegal activity—ranging from accounting fraud to using the Internet to steal another person's credit card number, from deceptive advertising of food and diet products to unfair competitive practices in the computer software industry—strengthen the public's perceptions that ethical standards and the level of trust in business need to be raised. Author David Callahan has commented, "Americans who wouldn't so much as shoplift a pack of chewing gum are committing felonies at tax time, betraying the trust of their patients, misleading investors, ripping off their insurance companies, lying to their clients, and much more."[8] Often, such charges start as ethical conflicts but evolve into legal disputes when cooperative conflict resolution cannot be accomplished. Headline-grabbing scandals like those associated with executive compensation and benefits packages create ethical concerns. It is estimated that the average CEO compensation is 204 times the amount paid to rank-and-file employees. This represents an increase in the compensation gap since 2009.[9] Consumer outrage over executive compensation is prompting companies to begin reevaluating how they compensate their CEOs relative to corporate performance. Walt Disney chairman and CEO Robert Iger saw a 15 percent drop in compensation after Disney failed to meet all its 2013 performance targets that the board had set.[10]

Actor Derek Hough attends Blue Jeans Go Green celebration of 1 Million pieces of denim collected for recycling, hosted by Miles Teller at SkyBar at the Mondrian Los Angeles on November 6, 2013 in West Hollywood, California.

However, it is important to understand that business ethics goes beyond legal issues. Ethical conduct builds trust among individuals and in business relationships, which validates and promotes confidence in business relationships. Establishing trust and confidence is much more difficult in organizations that have reputations for acting unethically. If you were to discover, for example, that a manager had misled you about company benefits when you were hired, your trust and confidence in that company would probably diminish. And if you learned that a colleague had lied to you about something, you probably would not trust or rely on that person in the future.

Ethical issues are not limited to for-profit organizations either. Ethical issues include all areas of organizational activities, including government. In government, several politicians and some high-ranking officials have faced disciplinary actions over ethical indiscretions. For instance, former New Orleans mayor Ray Nagin was found guilty of 20 counts of corruption. Allegations claim that he accepted more than $500,000 in bribes.[11] Even sports can be subject to ethical lapses. New York Yankees third baseman Alex Rodriguez was suspended after he was accused of using illegal testosterone lozenges before baseball games. However, Rodriguez continues to maintain his innocence.[12] Thus, whether made in science, politics, sports, or business, most decisions are judged as right or wrong, ethical or unethical. Negative judgments can affect an organization's ability to build relationships with customers and suppliers, attract investors, and retain employees.[13]

Although we will not tell you in this chapter what you ought to do, others—your superiors, co-workers, and family—will make judgments about the ethics of your actions and decisions. Learning how to recognize and resolve ethical issues is a key step in evaluating ethical decisions in business.

认识商业中的伦理问题
Recognizing Ethical Issues in Business

Recognizing ethical issues is the most important step in understanding business ethics. An **ethical issue** is an identifiable problem, situation, or opportunity that requires a person to choose from among several actions that may be evaluated as right or wrong, ethical or unethical. In business, such a choice often involves weighing monetary profit against what a person considers appropriate conduct. The best way to judge the ethics of a decision is to look at a situation from a customer's or competitor's viewpoint: Should liquid-diet manufacturers make unsubstantiated claims about their products? Should an engineer agree to divulge her former employer's trade secrets to

伦理问题
ethical issue
an identifiable problem, situation, or opportunity that requires a person to choose from among several actions that may be evaluated as right or wrong, ethical or unethical

Ralph Lauren reported that its subsidiary had bribed foreign officials in Argentina. Because it took quick action to address the misconduct, the compay did not face charges.

ensure that she gets a better job with a competitor? Should a salesperson omit facts about a product's poor safety record in his presentation to a customer? Such questions require the decision maker to evaluate the ethics of his or her choice.

Many business issues seem straightforward and easy to resolve on the surface, but are in reality very complex. A person often needs several years of experience in business to understand what is acceptable or ethical. For example, it is considered improper to give or accept **bribes,** which are payments, gifts, or special favors intended to influence the outcome of a decision. A bribe benefits an individual or a company at the expense of other stakeholders. Companies that do business overseas should be aware that bribes are a significant ethical issue and are, in fact, illegal in many countries. In the United States, the Foreign Corrupt Practices Act imposes heavy penalties on companies found guilty of bribery.

贿赂
bribes
payments, gifts, or special favors intended to influence the outcome of a decision

Ethics is also related to the culture in which a business operates. In the United States, for example, it would be inappropriate for a businessperson to bring an elaborately wrapped gift to a prospective client on their first meeting—the gift could be viewed as a bribe. In Japan, however, it is considered impolite *not* to bring a gift. Experience with the culture in which a business operates is critical to understanding what is ethical or unethical.

To help you understand ethical issues that perplex businesspeople today, we will take a brief look at some of them in this section. Ethical issues can be more complex now than in the past. The vast number of news-format investigative programs has increased consumer and employee awareness of organizational misconduct. In addition, the multitude of cable channels and Internet resources has improved the awareness of ethical problems among the general public.

One of the principal causes of unethical behavior in organizations is overly aggressive financial or business objectives. Many of these issues relate to decisions and concerns that managers have to deal with daily. It is not possible to discuss every issue, of course. However, a discussion of a few issues can help you begin to recognize the ethical problems with which businesspersons must deal. Many ethical issues in business can be categorized in the context of their relation with abusive and intimidating behavior, conflicts of interest, fairness and honesty, communications, misuse of company resources, and business associations. The National Business Ethics Survey found that workers witness many instances of ethical misconduct in their organizations (see Table 2.2).

滥用工作时间

Misuse of Company Time. Theft of time is a common area of misconduct observed in the workplace.[14] One example of misusing time in the workplace is by engaging in activities that are not necessary for the job. For instance, many employees spend an average of one hour each day using social networking sites or watching YouTube. In this case, the employee is misusing not only time but also company resources by using the company's computer and Internet access for personal use.[15] Time theft costs can be difficult to measure but are estimated to cost companies hundreds of billions of dollars annually. It is widely believed that the average employee "steals" 4.5 hours a week with late arrivals, leaving early, long lunch breaks,

TABLE 2.2
Percentage of U.S. Workforce Observing Specific Forms of Misconduct, 2011 and 2013

	2011 (%)	2013 (%)
Overall	45	41
Abusive behavior	21	18
Lying to employees	20	17
Conflict of interest	15	12
Violating company Internet use policies	16	12
Discrimination against employees	15	12
Violations of health or safety regulations	13	10
Lying to customers, vendors, the public	12	10
Retaliation against reporters of misconduct		10
Falsifying time reports/hours worked	12	10
Stealing or theft	12	9

Source: Ethics Resource Center, 2013 National Business Ethics Survey® of the U.S. Workforce *(Arlington, VA: Ethics Resource Center, 2014), pp. 41–42.*

inappropriate sick days, excessive socializing, and engaging in personal activities such as online shopping and watching sports while on the job. All of these activities add up to lost productivity and profits for the employer—and relate to ethical issues in the area of time theft.

侮辱和恐吓行为

Abusive and Intimidating Behavior. Abusive or intimidating behavior is the most common ethical problem for employees. These concepts can mean anything from physical threats, false accusations, profanity, insults, yelling, harshness, and unreasonableness to ignoring someone or simply being annoying; and the meaning of these words can differ by person—you probably have some ideas of your own. Abusive behavior can be placed on a continuum from a minor distraction to a disruption of the workplace. For example, what one person may define as yelling might be another's definition of normal speech. Civility in our society is a concern, and the workplace is no exception. The productivity level of many organizations has been diminished by the time spent unraveling abusive relationships.

The show *Undercover Boss* gives managers and business owners the chance to understand how their subordinates feel as they take on the responsibilities of their employees. Many bosses develop a stronger appreciation for their employees' challenging jobs, as Kat Cole, president of Cinnabon Inc., did after spending time undercover in the company's retail locations.

Abusive behavior is difficult to assess and manage because of diversity in culture and lifestyle. What does it mean to speak profanely? Is profanity only related to specific words or other such terms that are common in today's business world? If you are using words that are normal in your language but that others consider to be profanity, have you just insulted, abused, or disrespected them?

Within the concept of abusive behavior, intent should be a consideration. If the employee was trying to convey a compliment but the comment was considered abusive, then it was probably a mistake. The way a word is said (voice inflection) can be important. Add to this the fact that we now live in a multicultural environment—doing business and working with many different cultural groups—and the businessperson soon realizes the depth of the ethical and legal issues that may arise. There are problems of word meanings by age and within cultures. For example, an expression such as "Did you guys hook up last night?" can have various meanings, including some that could be considered offensive in a work environment.

Bullying is associated with a hostile workplace when a person or group is targeted and is threatened, harassed, belittled, verbally abused, or overly criticized. Bullying may create what some consider a hostile environment, a term generally associated with sexual harassment. Although sexual harassment has legal recourse, bullying has little legal recourse at this time. Bullying is a widespread problem in the United States, and can cause psychological damage that can result in health-endangering consequences to the target. Surveys reveal that bullying in the workplace is on the rise.[16] As Table 2.3 indicates, bullying can use a mix of verbal, nonverbal, and manipulative threatening expressions to damage workplace productivity. One may wonder why workers tolerate such activities. The problem is that 81 percent of workplace bullies are supervisors. Additionally, bullying can occur in any type of business. A bullying scandal at the Miami Dolphins involved a player who abruptly left the team after a hazing incident. The player claimed he had been bullied mercilessly by three starters on the Dolphins' offensive line, which harmed his mental well-being.[17]

滥用公司资源

Misuse of Company Resources. Misuse of company resources has been identified by the Ethics Resource Center as a leading issue in observed misconduct in organizations. Issues might include spending an excessive amount of time on personal e-mails, submitting personal expenses on company expense reports, or using the company copier for personal use. A senior administrative city government worker in New York was fired for misusing the company's work cell phone. It was estimated she spent an hour a day making personal calls, racketing up charges of $3,000.[18] While serious resource abuse can result in firing, some abuse can have legal repercussions.

TABLE 2.3
Actions Associated with Bullies

1.	Spreading rumors to damage others
2.	Blocking others' communication in the workplace
3.	Flaunting status or authority to take advantage of others
4.	Discrediting others' ideas and opinions
5.	Use of e-mails to demean others
6.	Failing to communicate or return communication
7.	Insults, yelling, and shouting
8.	Using terminology to discriminate by gender, race, or age
9.	Using eye or body language to hurt others or their reputation
10.	Taking credit for others' work or ideas

Source: © O. C. Ferrell, 2011.

A man from Reddick, Florida, was arrested after misusing his company credit card at gas stations. Investigations revealed he had used the card to purchase other people's gas and then had them pay him a reduced charge to pocket.[19]

The most common way that employees abuse resources is by using company computers for personal use. Typical examples of using a computer for personal use include shopping on the Internet, downloading music, doing personal banking, surfing the Internet for entertainment purposes, or visiting Facebook. Some companies have chosen to block certain sites such as YouTube or Pandora from employees. However, other companies choose to take a more flexible approach. For example, many have instituted policies that allow for some personal computer use as long as the use does not detract significantly from the workday.

No matter what approach a business chooses to take, it must have policies in place to prevent company resource abuse. Because misuse of company resources is such a widespread problem, many companies, like Boeing, have implemented official policies delineating acceptable use of company resources. Boeing's policy states that use of company resources is acceptable when it does not result in "significant added costs, disruption of business processes, or any other disadvantage to the company." The policy further states that use of company resources for noncompany purposes is acceptable only when an employee receives explicit permission to do so. This kind of policy is in line with that of many companies, particularly large ones that can easily lose millions of dollars and thousands of hours of productivity to these activities.[20]

利益冲突

Conflict of Interest. A conflict of interest, one of the most common ethical issues identified by employees, exists when a person must choose whether to advance his or her own personal interests or those of others. For example, a manager in a corporation is supposed to ensure that the company is profitable so that its stockholder-owners receive a return on their investment. In other words, the manager has a responsibility to investors. If she instead makes decisions that give her more power or money but do not help the company, then she has a conflict of interest—she is acting to benefit herself at the expense of her company and is not fulfilling her responsibilities as an employee. To avoid conflicts of interest, employees must be able to separate their personal financial interests from their business dealings. In the wake of the 2008 meltdown on Wall Street, stakeholders and legislators pushed for reform of the credit rating industry. Many cited rampant conflicts of interest between financial firms and the companies that rate them as part of the reason no one recognized the impending financial disaster. Conflict of interest has long been a serious problem in the financial industry because the financial companies pay the credit raters money in order to be rated. Because different rating companies exist, financial firms can also shop around for the best rating. There is no third-party mediator who oversees the financial industry and how firms are rated.[21]

Insider trading is an example of a conflict of interest. Insider trading is the buying or selling of stocks by insiders who possess material that is still not public. The Justice Department has taken an aggressive stance toward insider trading. For instance, SAC Capital Advisors LP settled with the Justice Department for $1.8 billion and agreed to close its investment advisory business after pleading guilty to insider trading. Several key executives at SAC Capital Advisors have been convicted of insider trading charges.[22] Bribery can also be a conflict of interest. While bribery is an increasing issue in many countries, it is more prevalent in some countries than in others. Transparency International has developed a Corruption Perceptions Index (Table 2.4). Note that there are 18 countries perceived as less corrupt than the United States.[23]

TABLE 2.4
Least Corrupt Countries

Rank	Country	CPI Score*
1.	Denmark/New Zealand	91
3.	Finland/Sweden	89
5.	Norway/Singapore	86
7.	Switzerland	85
8.	Netherlands	83
9.	Australia/Canada	81
11.	Luxembourg	80
12.	Germany/Iceland	78
14.	United Kingdom	76
15.	Barbados/Belgium	75
18.	Japan	74
19.	United States/Uruguay	73

**Corruption Perceptions Index (CPI) score relates to perceptions of the degree of public sector corruption as seen by businesspeople and country analysts and ranges between 0 (highly corrupt) and 10 (very clean).*

Source: Corruption Perceptions Index 2013, *Copyright Transparency International 2013.*

公正与诚实
Fairness and Honesty

Fairness and honesty are at the heart of business ethics and relate to the general values of decision makers. At a minimum, businesspersons are expected to follow all applicable laws and regulations. But beyond obeying the law, they are expected not to harm customers, employees, clients, or competitors knowingly through deception, misrepresentation, coercion, or discrimination. Honesty and fairness can relate to how the employees use the resources of the organization. In contrast, dishonesty is usually associated with a lack of integrity, lack of disclosure, and lying. One common example of dishonesty is theft of office supplies. Fraud and theft occurs at approximately 35 percent of small businesses.[24] Although the majority of office supply thefts involve small things such as pencils or Post-it Notes, some workers admit to stealing more expensive equipment such as laptops, PDAs, and cell phones. Employees should be aware of policies on taking items and recognize how these decisions relate to ethical behavior.

One aspect of fairness relates to competition. Although numerous laws have been passed to foster competition and make monopolistic practices illegal, companies sometimes gain control over markets by using questionable practices that harm competition. Bullying can also occur between companies that are intense competitors. For example, European antitrust regulators alleged that some of the world's biggest banks—including Goldman Sachs, Morgan Stanley, and J.P. Morgan—collaborated with an industry association to prevent exchanges from offering and trading in credit derivatives. The allegations claim that the collusion was done to prevent banks from losing revenue in this profitable area. If true, the banks would be in violation of European laws dictating fair competition. The banks vehemently denied the accusations.[25] In many cases, the alleged misconduct not only can have monetary and legal implications but can also threaten reputation, investor confidence, and customer

Misuse of company time through the use of personal social media is very costly to businesses.

loyalty. At the minimum, a business found guilty of anticompetitive practices will be forced to stop such conduct. However, many companies end up paying millions in penalties to settle allegations.[26]

Another aspect of fairness and honesty relates to disclosure of potential harm caused by product use. For instance, the FDA has become increasingly concerned about the use of trans fats in food. The FDA believes that disclosing trans fats through labeling is no longer sufficient. Because trans fats are considered to be harmful, the FDA announced a proposal to phase out trans fats. If this proposal takes effect, food companies would have to eliminate trans fats from their ingredients or petition the agency and meet strong safety standards.[27]

Dishonesty has become a significant problem in the United States. A survey of 23,000 high school students reported that 51 percent of students admitted to cheating on an exam at least once in the past year, and 20 percent admitted to stealing. Perhaps even more disturbing, 93 percent of respondents stated that they were satisfied with their personal ethical character. If today's students are tomorrow's leaders, there is likely to be a correlation between acceptable behavior today and tomorrow. This adds to the argument that the leaders of today must be prepared for the ethical risks associated with this downward trend.[28]

Even military officers have felt the pressure to cheat. At one Air Force base in Montana, nearly half of the Air Force officers at the base cheated on a proficiency exam. Another investigation was launched shortly afterward to determine whether senior Navy enlistees in South Carolina cheated on an exam containing classified

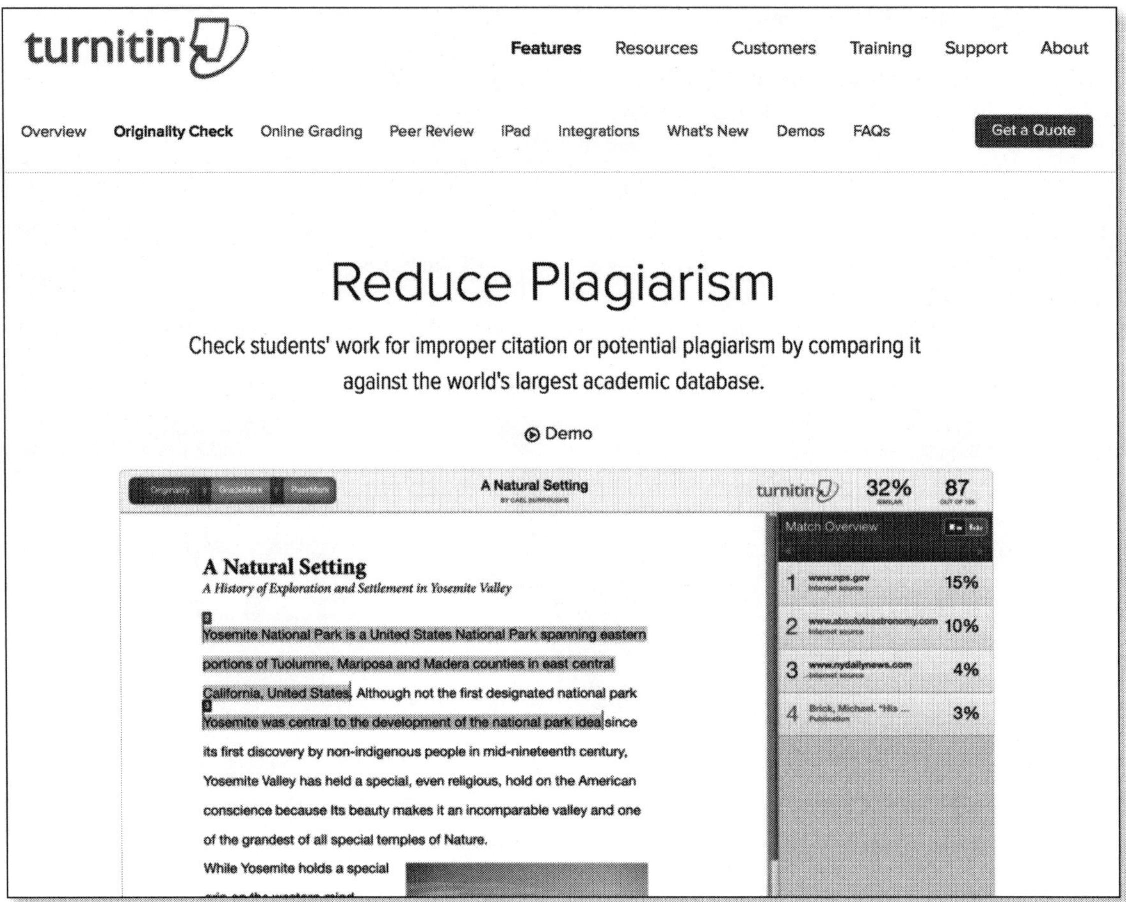

TrunltIn is an Internet service that allows teachers to determine if their students have plagriarized content.

information. Another 800 soldiers in the Army were placed under criminal investigation for being involved in kickbacks to soldiers who recruited friends. As a result of these scandals, the military is increasing its ethics training.[29]

沟通

Communications. Communications is another area in which ethical concerns may arise. False and misleading advertising, as well as deceptive personal-selling tactics, anger consumers and can lead to the failure of a business. Truthfulness about product safety and quality is also important to consumers. General Motors (GM) issued a recall on its 2005–2007 Chevrolet Cobalt vehicles, but not until at least six deaths were attributed to Cobalt car accidents where the airbags did not deploy due to switch failure. It has been alleged that a GM engineer had encountered the problem as early as 2004, but GM did not issue a recall. Rather, the company sent a service bulletin to its dealers advising them to install snap-on key covers that would fix the problem if customers complained. Many dealers did not install these key covers. A congressional hearing was ordered to investigate the situation, but before GM testified, it launched an additional recall of 1.5 million vehicles for electric power steering issues.[30]

Some companies fail to provide enough information for consumers about differences or similarities between products. For example, driven by high prices for medicines, many consumers are turning to Canadian, Mexican, and overseas Internet sources for drugs to treat a variety of illnesses and conditions. However, research suggests that a significant percentage of these imported pharmaceuticals may not actually contain the labeled drug, and the counterfeit drugs could even be harmful to those who take them.[31]

New York Yankees third baseman Alex Rodriguez was suspended after evidence suggested he had been using performance-enhancing drugs.

Another important aspect of communications that may raise ethical concerns relates to product labeling. This becomes an even greater concern with potentially harmful products like cigarettes. In Europe, at least 30 percent of the front side of cigarette packaging and 40 percent of the back needs to be taken up by the warning. The FDA passed similar rules for the United States, but its ruling was blocked until the lawsuit between the FDA and cigarette companies is resolved.[32] However, labeling of other products raises ethical questions when it threatens basic rights, such as freedom of speech and expression. This is the heart of the controversy surrounding the movement to require warning labels on movies and videogames, rating their content, language, and appropriate audience age. Although people in the entertainment industry claim that such labeling violates their First Amendment right to freedom of expression, other consumers—particularly parents—believe that labeling is needed to protect children from harmful influences. Similarly, alcoholic beverage and cigarette manufacturers have argued that a total ban on cigarette and alcohol advertisements violates the First Amendment. Internet regulation, particularly that designed to protect children and the elderly, is on the forefront in consumer protection legislation. Because of the debate surrounding the acceptability of these business activities, they remain major ethical issues.

商业关系

Business Relationships. The behavior of businesspersons toward customers, suppliers, and others in their workplace may also generate ethical concerns. Ethical behavior within a business involves keeping company secrets, meeting obligations and responsibilities, and avoiding undue pressure that may force others to act unethically.

Managers in particular, because of the authority of their position, have the opportunity to influence employees' actions. For example, a manager might influence employees to use pirated computer software to save costs. The use of illegal software puts the employee and the company at legal risk, but employees may feel pressured to do so by their superior's authority. The National Business Ethics Survey found that employees who feel pressured to compromise ethical standards view top and middle managers as the greatest source of such pressure.[33]

It is the responsibility of managers to create a work environment that helps the organization achieve its objectives and fulfill its responsibilities. However, the methods that managers use to enforce these responsibilities should not compromise employee rights. Organizational pressures may encourage a person to engage in activities that he or she might otherwise view as unethical, such as invading others' privacy or stealing a competitor's secrets. The firm may provide only vague or lax supervision on ethical issues, creating the opportunity for misconduct. Managers who offer no ethical direction to employees create many opportunities for manipulation, dishonesty, and conflicts of interest.

TABLE 2.5
Questions to Consider in Determining Whether an Action Is Ethical

Are there any potential legal restrictions or violations that could result from the action?
Does your company have a specific code of ethics or policy on the action?
Is this activity customary in your industry? Are there any industry trade groups that provide guidelines or codes of conduct that address this issue?
Would this activity be accepted by your co-workers? Will your decision or action withstand open discussion with co-workers and managers and survive untarnished?
How does this activity fit with your own beliefs and values?

剽窃
plagiarism
the act of taking someone else's work and presenting it as your own without mentioning the source

Plagiarism—taking someone else's work and presenting it as your own without mentioning the source—is another ethical issue. As a student, you may be familiar with plagiarism in school—for example, copying someone else's term paper or quoting from a published work or Internet source without acknowledging it. In business, an ethical issue arises when an employee copies reports or takes the work or ideas of others and presents it as his or her own. A manager attempting to take credit for a subordinate's ideas is engaging in another type of plagiarism.

就伦理问题做出决定
Making Decisions about Ethical Issues

Although we've presented a variety of ethical issues that may arise in business, it can be difficult to recognize specific ethical issues in practice. Whether a decision maker recognizes an issue as an ethical one often depends on the issue itself. Managers, for example, tend to be more concerned about issues that affect those close to them, as well as issues that have immediate rather than long-term consequences. Thus, the perceived importance of an ethical issue substantially affects choices. However, only a few issues receive scrutiny, and most receive no attention at all.[34]

Table 2.5 lists some questions you may want to ask yourself and others when trying to determine whether an action is ethical. Open discussion of ethical issues does not eliminate ethical problems, but it does promote both trust and learning in an organization.[35] When people feel that they cannot discuss what they are doing with their co-workers or superiors, there is a good chance that an ethical issue exists. Once a person has recognized an ethical issue and can openly discuss it with others, he or she has begun the process of resolving that issue.

LO 2-3

改善商业的道德行为
Improving Ethical Behavior in Business

Understanding how people make ethical choices and what prompts a person to act unethically may reverse the current trend toward unethical behavior in business. Ethical decisions in an organization are influenced by three key factors: individual moral standards, the influence of managers and co-workers, and the opportunity to engage in misconduct (Figure 2.2). While you have great control over your personal ethics

FIGURE 2.2
Three Factors That Influence Business Ethics

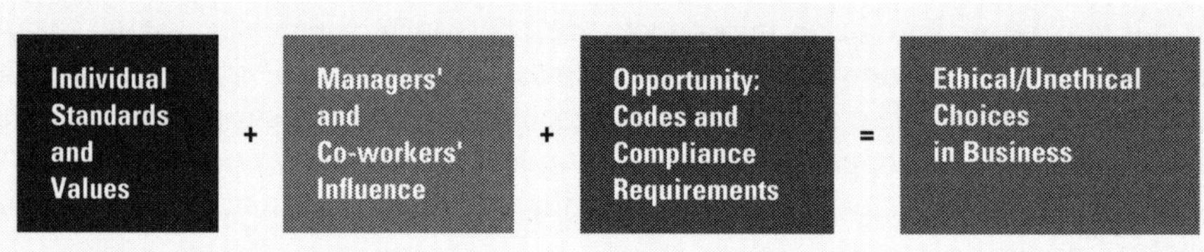

Consider Ethics and Social Responsibility

Ralph Lauren Sets Example in FCPA Case

What does a company do when an internal audit finds that bribery has occurred? For Ralph Lauren Corporation, it turns itself in. The company discovered that from 2005 to 2009, bribes were paid to customs and government officials in Argentina in the form of cash, dresses, handbags, and perfume to expedite processes of merchandise in the South American country. This misconduct violates the Foreign Corrupt Practices Act (FCPA), which makes it illegal for companies with operations in the United States to bribe foreign officials.

When Ralph Lauren discovered the bribery, it immediately reported the misconduct to the Securities and Exchange Commission (SEC) and worked with government authorities in the investigation. The company agreed to pay $1.6 million to settle investigations. More than $700,000 of this payment covers the amount of the bribes paid to officials.

By turning itself in, Ralph Lauren received applause from several SEC officials, who deemed the company's actions ethical. The clothing retailer was able to resolve charges and sign nonprosecution agreements. This was the first such agreement in history related to the FCPA. This case demonstrates that it pays to comply with the law when misconduct is discovered. Not only can penalties be less severe, but Ralph Lauren's reputation as a company committed to doing the right thing will likely improve.[36]

Discussion Questions

1. How did Ralph Lauren violate the FCPA?
2. Why did Ralph Lauren receive less severe penalties for the misconduct?
3. How can the Ralph Lauren bribery case set a precedent for other firms when discovering misconduct?

outside the workplace, your co-workers and superiors exert significant control over your choices at work through authority and example. In fact, the activities and examples set by co-workers, along with rules and policies established by the firm, are critical in gaining consistent ethical compliance in an organization. If the company fails to provide good examples and direction for appropriate conduct, confusion and conflict will develop and result in the opportunity for misconduct. If your boss or co-workers leave work early, you may be tempted to do so as well. If you see co-workers engaged in personal activities such as shopping online or watching YouTube, then you may be more likely to do so also. In addition, having sound personal values contributes to an ethical workplace.

Because ethical issues often emerge from conflict, it is useful to examine the causes of ethical conflict. Business managers and employees often experience some tension between their own ethical beliefs and their obligations to the organizations in which they work. Many employees utilize different ethical standards at work than they do at home. This conflict increases when employees feel that their company is encouraging unethical conduct or exerting pressure on them to engage in it.

It is difficult for employees to determine what conduct is acceptable within a company if the firm does not have established ethics policies and standards. And without such policies and standards, employees may base decisions on how their peers and superiors behave. Professional **codes of ethics** are formalized rules and standards that describe what the company expects of its employees. Codes of ethics do not have to be so detailed that they take into account every situation, but they should provide guidelines and principles that can help employees achieve organizational objectives and address risks in an acceptable and ethical way. The development of a code of ethics should include not only a firm's executives and board of directors, but also legal staff and employees from all areas of a firm.[37] Table 2.6 lists some key things to consider when developing a code of ethics.

道德准则
codes of ethics
formalized rules and standards that describe what a company expects of its employees

TABLE 2.6
Key Things to Consider in Developing a Code of Ethics

• Create a team to assist with the process of developing the code (include management and nonmanagement employees from across departments and functions).
• Solicit input from employees from different departments, functions, and regions to compile a list of common questions and answers to include in the code document.
• Make certain that the headings of the code sections can be easily understood by all employees.
• Avoid referencing specific U.S. laws and regulations or those of specific countries, particularly for codes that will be distributed to employees in multiple regions.
• Hold employee group meetings on a complete draft version (including graphics and pictures) of the text, using language that everyone can understand.
• Inform employees that they will receive a copy of the code during an introduction session.
• Let all employees know that they will receive future ethics training that will, in part, cover the important information contained in the code document.

Source: Adapted from William Miller, "Implementing an Organizational Code of Ethics," International Business Ethics Review *7 (Winter 2004), pp. 1, 6–10.*

Codes of ethics, policies on ethics, and ethics training programs advance ethical behavior because they prescribe which activities are acceptable and which are not, and they limit the opportunity for misconduct by providing punishments for violations of the rules and standards. Codes and policies on ethics encourage the creation of an ethical culture in the company. According to the National Business Ethics Survey (NBES), employees in organizations that have written codes of conduct and ethics training, ethics offices or hotlines, and systems for reporting are more likely to report misconduct when they observe it. The survey found that a company's ethical culture is the greatest determinant of future misconduct.[38]

The enforcement of ethical codes and policies through rewards and punishments increases the acceptance of ethical standards by employees. For instance, Texas Instruments has a strong code of ethics and a culture of corporate citizenship that encourages employee participation. Every year, the firm releases an ethics and citizenship report and exercises transparency by making it easily accessible through its website. Texas Instruments posts periodic updates on its citizenship activities throughout the year, and a brochure featuring its values and ethical expectations can also be downloaded from its website. The company has been selected by the Ethisphere Institute as one of the world's most ethical companies for seven consecutive years.[39]

检举
whistleblowing
the act of an employee exposing an employer's wrongdoing to outsiders, such as the media or government regulatory agencies

One of the most important components of an ethics program is a means through which employees can report observed misconduct anonymously. Although the risk of retaliation is still a major factor in whether an employee will report illegal conduct, the NBES found that whistleblowing has increased in the past few years. Approximately 63 percent of respondents said they reported misconduct when they observed it.[40] **Whistleblowing** occurs when an employee exposes an employer's wrongdoing to outsiders, such as the media or government regulatory agencies. However, more companies are establishing programs to encourage employees to report illegal or unethical practices internally so that they can take steps to remedy problems before they result in legal action or generate negative publicity.

Unfortunately, whistleblowers are often treated negatively in organizations. The government seeks to discourage this practice by rewarding firms that encourage employees to report misconduct—with reduced fines and penalties when violations occur. Congress has also taken steps to close a legislative loophole in whistleblowing legislation that has led to the dismissal of many whistleblowers. In 2010, Congress passed the Dodd-Frank Act, which includes a "whistleblower bounty program." The Securities and Exchange Commission can now award whistleblowers between 10 and 30 percent of monetary sanctions over $1 million. The hope is that incentives will encourage more people to come forward with information regarding corporate misconduct.

The current trend is to move away from legally based ethical initiatives in organizations to cultural- or integrity-based initiatives that make ethics a part of core organizational values. Organizations recognize that effective business ethics programs are good for business performance. Firms that develop higher levels of trust function more efficiently and effectively and avoid damaged company reputations and product images. Organizational ethics initiatives have been supportive of many positive and diverse organizational objectives, such as profitability, hiring, employee satisfaction, and customer loyalty.[41] Conversely, lack of organizational ethics initiatives and the absence of workplace values such as honesty, trust, and integrity can have a negative impact on organizational objectives and employee retention. According to one study, three of the most common factors that executives give for why turnover increases are employee loss of trust in the company, a lack of transparency among company leaders, and unfair employee treatment.[42]

社会责任的本质
The Nature of Social Responsibility

LO 2-4

For the purposes of this book, we classify four stages of social responsibility: financial, legal compliance, ethics, and philanthropy (Table 2.7). Another way of categorizing these four dimensions of social responsibility: economic, legal, ethical, and voluntary (including philanthropic).[43] Earning profits is the economic foundation, and complying with the law is the next step. However, a business whose *sole* objective is to maximize profits is not likely to consider its social responsibility, although its activities will probably be legal. (We looked at ethical responsibilities in the first half of this chapter.) Finally, voluntary responsibilities are additional activities that may

TABLE 2.7
Social Responsibility Requirements

Stages	Examples
Stage 1: Financial Viability	Starbucks offers investors a healthy return on investment, including paying dividends.
Stage 2: Compliance with Legal and Regulatory Requirements	Starbucks specifies in its code of conduct that payments made to foreign government officials must be lawful according to the laws of the United States and the foreign country.
Stage 3: Ethics, Principles, and Values	Starbucks offers healthcare benefits to part-time employees and supports coffee growers by offering them fair prices.
Stage 4: Philanthropic Activities	Starbucks created the Starbucks Foundation to award grants to eligible nonprofits and to give back to their communities.

not be required but which promote human welfare or goodwill. Legal and economic concerns have long been acknowledged in business, but voluntary and ethical issues are more recent concerns.

企业公民
corporate citizenship the extent to which businesses meet the legal, ethical, economic, and voluntary responsibilities placed on them by their stakeholders

Corporate citizenship is the extent to which businesses meet the legal, ethical, economic, and voluntary responsibilities placed on them by their various stakeholders. It involves the activities and organizational processes adopted by businesses to meet their social responsibilities. A commitment to corporate citizenship by a firm indicates a strategic focus on fulfilling the social responsibilities expected of it by its stakeholders. For example, CVS is attempting to demonstrate corporate citizenship by eliminating tobacco products from its pharmacies. Although this will cost the firm $2 billion in sales, CVS believes it is contradictory to market itself as a health care services business while still selling a dangerous product.[44] Corporate citizenship involves action and measurement of the extent to which a firm embraces the corporate citizenship philosophy and then follows through by implementing citizenship and social responsibility initiatives. One of the major corporate citizenship issues is the focus on preserving the environment. The majority of people agree that climate change is a global emergency, but there is no agreement on how to solve the problem.[45] Another example of a corporate citizenship issue might be animal rights—an issue that is important to many stakeholders. As the organic and local foods movements grow and become more profitable, more and more stakeholders are calling for more humane practices in factory farms as well.[46] Large factory farms are where most Americans get their meat, but some businesses are looking at more animal-friendly options in response to public outcry.

connect
Need help Understanding Social Responsibility? Visit your Connect ebook video tab for a brief animated explanation.

Part of the answer to the climate change crisis is alternative energy such as solar, wind, bio-fuels, and hydro applications. The drive for alternative fuels such as ethanol from corn has added new issues such as food price increases and food shortages. More than 2 billion consumers earn less than $2 a day in wages. Sharply increased food costs have led to riots and government policies to restrict trade in basic commodities such as rice, corn, and soybeans.[47]

To respond to these developments, most companies are introducing eco-friendly products and marketing efforts. Netherlands-based Royal Philips has released its second generation of 75-watt and 100-watt LED equivalent light bulbs. To demonstrate their sustainability, these bulbs have been ENERGY STAR certified. LEDs are a more sustainable alternative to incandescent light bulbs, but they are more costly to the consumer. In its desires to make adoption easier for consumers, Philips offered rebates of up to $10 per light bulb.[48] However, although 69 percent of consumers say it is all right for a firm not to be environmentally perfect as long as it is honest, 78 percent claim that they will boycott firms caught making misleading environmental claims.[49] This is because many businesses are promoting themselves as green-conscious and concerned about the environment without actually making the necessary commitments to environmental health.

The Ethisphere Institute selects an annual list of the world's most ethical companies based on the following criteria: corporate citizenship and responsibility; corporate governance; innovation that contributes to the public well-being; industry leadership; executive leadership and tone from the top; legal, regulatory, and reputation track record; and internal systems and ethics/compliance program.[50] Table 2.8 shows 26 from that list.

Although the concept of social responsibility is receiving more and more attention, it is still not universally accepted. Table 2.9 lists some of the arguments for and against social responsibility.

TABLE 2.8
A Selection of the World's Most Ethical Companies

L'OREAL	eBay
Starbucks Coffee Company	Hospital Corporation of America (HCA)
Marks and Spencer	Xerox Corporation
General Electric Company	Eaton
T-Mobile USA Inc.	Cummins
PepsiCo	Ford Motor Company
ManpowerGroup	Google Inc.
Colgate-Palmolive Company	Gap, Inc.
International Paper	Texas Instruments Incorporated
Adobe Systems Incorporated	Waste Management
UPS	Kellogg Company
Accenture	Aflac Incorporated
Salesforce.com	Safeway Inc.

Source: "2014 World's Most Ethical Companies—Honorees," Ethisphere.

TABLE 2.9
The Arguments For and Against Social Responsibility

For:
1. Business helped to create many of the social problems that exist today, so it should play a significant role in solving them, especially in the areas of pollution reduction and cleanup.
2. Businesses should be more responsible because they have the financial and technical resources to help solve social problems.
3. As members of society, businesses should do their fair share to help others.
4. Socially responsible decision making by businesses can prevent increased government regulation.
5. Social responsibility is necessary to ensure economic survival: If businesses want educated and healthy employees, customers with money to spend, and suppliers with quality goods and services in years to come, they must take steps to help solve the social and environmental problems that exist today.
Against:
1. It sidetracks managers from the primary goal of business—earning profits. Every dollar donated to social causes or otherwise spent on society's problems is a dollar less for owners and investors.
2. Participation in social programs gives businesses greater power, perhaps at the expense of particular segments of society.
3. Some people question whether business has the expertise needed to assess and make decisions about social problems.
4. Many people believe that social problems are the responsibility of government agencies and officials, who can be held accountable by voters.

社会责任问题
Social Responsibility Issues

As with ethics, managers consider social responsibility on a daily basis. Among the many social issues that managers must consider are their firms' relations with owners and stockholders, employees, consumers, the environment, and the community. For example, Indra Nooyi, CEO of PepsiCo, believes that companies must embrace "purpose," not just for financial results, but also for the imprint they leave on society. She goes on to say that stakeholders, including employees, consumers, and regulators, "will leave no doubt that performance without purpose is not a long-term sustainable formula."[51]

Social responsibility is a dynamic area with issues changing constantly in response to society's demands. There is much evidence that social responsibility is associated with improved business performance. Consumers are refusing to buy from businesses that receive publicity about misconduct. A number of studies have found a direct relationship between social responsibility and profitability, as well as a link that exists between employee commitment and customer loyalty—two major concerns of any firm trying to increase profits.[52] This section highlights a few of the many social responsibility issues that managers face; as managers become aware of and work toward the solution of current social problems, new ones will certainly emerge.

与所有者和股东的关系

Relations with Owners and Stockholders. Businesses must first be responsible to their owners, who are primarily concerned with earning a profit or a return on their investment in a company. In a small business, this responsibility is fairly easy to fulfill because the owner(s) personally manages the business or knows the managers well. In larger businesses, particularly corporations owned by thousands of stockholders, ensuring responsibility becomes a more difficult task.

A business's obligations to its owners and investors, as well as to the financial community at large, include maintaining proper accounting procedures, providing all relevant information to investors about the current and projected performance of the firm, and protecting the owners' rights and investments. In short, the business must maximize the owners' investments in the firm.

与员工的关系

Employee Relations. Another issue of importance to a business is its responsibilities to employees. Without employees, a business cannot carry out its goals. Employees expect businesses to provide a safe workplace, pay them adequately for their work, and keep them informed of what is happening in their company. They want employers to listen to their grievances and treat them fairly. For instance, after months of negotiations, Safeway and Giant Food supermarkets agreed to a three-year agreement with the United Food & Commercial Workers union to continue providing health care benefits and pensions to workers. However, the decision did not come easily. The union nearly organized a worker strike when the stores could not agree on a new contract, especially as there was talk that the supermarkets were considering eliminating health care benefits for part-time workers and spouses. The agreement with the union will likely contribute to higher morale among employees.[53]

Congress has passed several laws regulating safety in the workplace, many of which are enforced by the Occupational Safety and Health Administration (OSHA). Labor unions have also made significant contributions to achieving safety in the workplace and improving wages and benefits. Most organizations now recognize that the safety and satisfaction of their employees are critical ingredients in their success, and many strive to go beyond what is legally expected of them. Healthy, satisfied employees also supply more than just labor to their employers. Employers are beginning to realize the importance of obtaining input from even the lowest-level employees to help the company reach its objectives.

A major social responsibility for business is providing equal opportunities for all employees regardless of their sex, age, race, religion, or nationality. Women and minorities have been slighted in the past in terms of education, employment, and advancement opportunities; additionally, many of their needs have not been addressed by business. Discrimination still occurs in business. The Equal Employment Opportunity Commission (EEOC) filed a class age discrimination lawsuit against Ruby Tuesday for discriminating against employees 40 years or older in several of its locations. Ruby Tuesday paid $575,000 and committed toward audits and better training as part of the settlement.[54] Women, who continue to bear most child-rearing responsibilities, often experience conflict between those responsibilities and their duties as employees. Consequently, day care has become a major employment issue for women, and more companies are providing day care facilities as part of their effort to recruit and advance women in the workforce. In addition, companies are considering alternative scheduling such as flex-time and job sharing to accommodate employee concerns. Telecommuting has grown significantly over the past 5 to 10 years as well. Many Americans today believe business has a social obligation to provide special opportunities for women and minorities to improve their standing in society.

与顾客的关系

Consumer Relations. A critical issue in business today is business's responsibility to customers, who look to business to provide them with satisfying, safe products and to respect their rights as consumers. The activities that independent individuals, groups, and organizations undertake to protect their rights as consumers are known as **consumerism.** To achieve their objectives, consumers and their advocates write letters to companies, lobby government agencies, make public service announcements, and boycott companies whose activities they deem irresponsible.

用户至上主义
consumerism
the activities that independent individuals, groups, and organizations undertake to protect their rights as consumers

Many of the desires of those involved in the consumer movement have a foundation in John F. Kennedy's 1962 consumer bill of rights, which highlighted four rights. The *right to safety* means that a business must not knowingly sell anything that could result in personal injury or harm to consumers. Defective or dangerous products erode public confidence in the ability of business to serve society. They also result in expensive litigation that ultimately increases the cost of products for all consumers. The right to safety also means businesses must provide a safe place for consumers to shop.

The *right to be informed* gives consumers the freedom to review complete information about a product before they buy it. This means that detailed information about ingredients, risks, and instructions for use are to be printed on labels and packages. When companies mislead consumers about the benefits of their products, then they infringe on consumers' rights to be informed. American Express Corporation paid $76 million to settle allegations that it had misled consumers about the benefits of its identity-theft protection add-on services.[55] The *right to choose* ensures that consumers have access to a variety of goods and services at competitive prices. The assurance of both satisfactory quality and service at a fair price is also a part of the consumer's right to choose. The *right to be heard* assures consumers that their interests will receive full and sympathetic consideration when the government formulates policy. It also ensures the fair treatment of consumers who voice complaints about a purchased product.

The role of the Federal Trade Commission's Bureau of Consumer Protection exists to protect consumers against unfair, deceptive, or fraudulent practices. The bureau, which enforces a variety of consumer protection laws, is divided into five divisions. The Division of Enforcement monitors legal compliance and investigates violations of

The National Hockey League's NHL Green iniatiative partners with organizations to contribute toward improving the environment.

laws, including unfulfilled holiday delivery promises by online shopping sites, employment opportunities fraud, scholarship scams, misleading advertising for health care products, and more.

可持续性问题

Sustainability Issues. Most people probably associate the term *environment* with nature, including wildlife, trees, oceans, and mountains. Until the 20th century, people generally thought of the environment solely in terms of how these resources could be harnessed to satisfy their needs for food, shelter, transportation, and recreation. As the earth's population swelled throughout the 20th century, however, humans began to use more and more of these resources and, with technological advancements, to do so with ever-greater efficiency. Although these conditions have resulted in a much-improved standard of living, they come with a cost. Plant and animal species, along with wildlife habitats, are disappearing at an accelerated rate, while pollution has rendered the atmosphere of some cities a gloomy haze. How to deal with these issues has become a major concern for business and society in the 21st century.

Although the scope of the word *sustainability* is broad, in this book we discuss the term from a strategic business perspective. Thus, we define **sustainability** as conducting activities in such a way as to provide for the long-term well-being of the natural environment, including all biological entities. Sustainability involves the interaction among nature and individuals, organizations, and business strategies and includes the assessment and improvement of business strategies, economic sectors, work practices, technologies, and lifestyles, so that they maintain the health of the natural environment. In recent years, business has played a significant role in adapting, using, and maintaining the quality of sustainability.

可持续性
sustainability
conducting activities in a way that allows for the long-term well-being of the natural environment, including all biological entities. Sustainability involves the assessment and improvement of business strategies, economic sectors, work practices, technologies, and lifestyles so that they maintain the health of the natural environment.

Environmental protection emerged as a major issue in the 20th century in the face of increasing evidence that pollution, uncontrolled use of natural resources, and population growth were putting increasing pressure on the long-term sustainability of these resources. Governments around the globe responded with environmental protection laws during the 1970s. In recent years, companies have been increasingly incorporating these issues into their overall business strategies. Some nonprofit organizations have stepped forward to provide leadership in gaining the cooperation of diverse groups in responsible environmental activities. For example, the Coalition for Environmentally Responsible Economies (CERES)—a union of businesses, consumer groups, environmentalists, and other stakeholders—has established a set of goals for environmental performance.

In the following section, we examine some of the most significant sustainability and environmental health issues facing business and society today, including pollution and alternative energy.

污染

Pollution. A major issue in the area of environmental responsibility is pollution. Water pollution results from dumping toxic chemicals and raw sewage into rivers and oceans, oil spills, and the burial of industrial waste in the ground where it may filter into underground water supplies. Fertilizers and insecticides used in farming and grounds maintenance also run off into water supplies with each rainfall. Water pollution problems are especially notable in heavily industrialized areas. Medical waste—such as used syringes, vials of blood, and HIV-contaminated materials—has turned up on beaches in New York, New Jersey, and Massachusetts, as well as other places. Society is demanding that water supplies be clean and healthful to reduce the potential danger from these substances.

Air pollution is usually the result of smoke and other pollutants emitted by manufacturing facilities, as well as carbon monoxide and hydrocarbons emitted by motor vehicles. In addition to the health risks posed by air pollution, when some chemical compounds emitted by manufacturing facilities react with air and rain, acid rain results. Acid rain has contributed to the deaths of many forests and lakes in North America as well as in Europe. Air pollution may also contribute to global warming; as carbon dioxide collects in the earth's atmosphere, it traps the sun's heat and prevents the earth's surface from cooling. It is indisputable that the global surface temperature has been increasing over the past 35 years. Worldwide passenger vehicle ownership has been growing due to rapid industrialization and consumer purchasing power in China, India, and other developing countries with large populations. The most important way to contain climate change is to control carbon emissions. The move to green buildings, higher-mileage cars, and other emissions reductions resulting from better efficiency have the potential to generate up to 50 percent of the reductions needed to keep warming at no more than 28°C above present temperatures—considered the "safe" level.[56] The 2007 U.S. Federal Energy bill raised average fuel economy (CAFE) standards to 35 mpg for cars by 2020, while Europe has the goal of a 40 mpg standard by the same deadline. Because buildings create half of U.S. greenhouse emissions, there is tremendous opportunity to develop conservation measures. For example, some utilities charge more for electricity in peak demand periods, which encourages behavioral changes that reduce consumption. More and more consumers are recognizing the need to protect the planet. Figure 2.3 shows the conservation habits of consumers when they purchase, use, and dispose of products. Although most consumers admit that sustainable products are important and that they bear responsibility for properly using and disposing of the product, many admit that they fail to do this.

FIGURE 2.3 Conservation Behaviors of Consumers

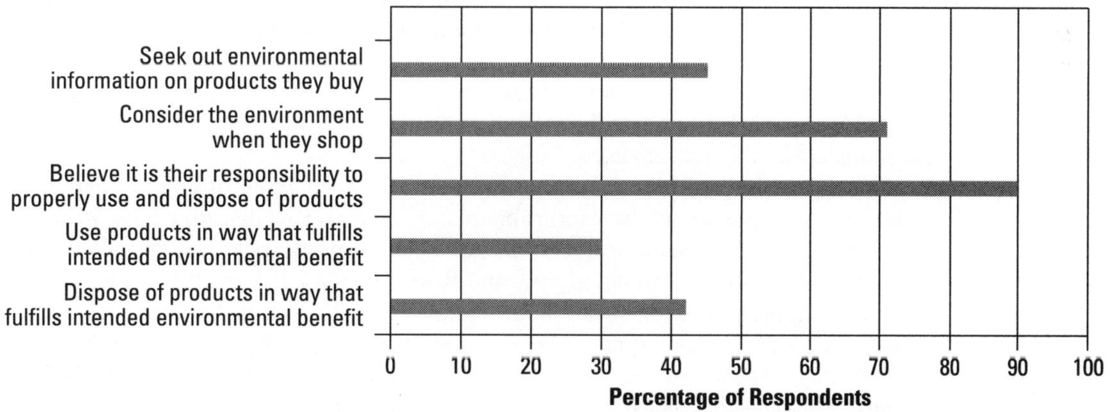

Online survey conducted March 7–10, 2013, by ORC International among a demographically representative sample of 1,068 adults, comprising 552 men and 516 women 18 years of age and older. The margin of error associated with a sample of this size is ±3% at a 95% level of confidence.

Source: Cone Communications, "Cone Releases 2013 Cone Communications Green Gap Trend Tracker," April 2, 2013.

Going Green

Sustainability Trade-offs: Lighter Vehicles and Higher Prices

As auto manufacturers focus on sustainability, vehicles are evolving into lighter versions of their old selves. Producing vehicles with materials such as aluminum, carbon fiber, and high-strength steel are decreasing the weight of vehicles by about 200 pounds, while still providing the same amount of strength and without increasing the retail price. It is estimated that a vehicle's weight accounts for two-thirds of the energy it uses, and lighter vehicles are expected to cut fuel usage in half. The use of lighter materials also allows for vehicles to be bound with structural adhesives and sealants, which can add rigidity to the body of the vehicle, absorb shock, and potentially provide a safer ride for the customer.

However, there is a downside. As cars become lighter, consumers face higher repair costs when it comes time to repair their environmentally friendly vehicles. These lighter materials are difficult to repair because welding and cutting weaken the surface. For example, customers may have to purchase an entire new panel for the damaged portion of the vehicle, which is more expensive than paying for repair work or replacement parts. Additionally, there have been cases wherein the auto adhesives have melted when reaching certain temperatures. These are some examples of the kinds of trade-offs companies and consumers are facing in the quest to be more sustainable.[57]

Discussion Questions

1. Discuss some of the trade-offs of having lighter, more sustainable vehicles.
2. Discuss any ethical issues you can identify in this scenario.
3. In light of the negative consequences of producing these vehicles, do you think companies should continue to produce lighter-weight vehicles in the name of sustainability? Why or why not?

Land pollution is tied directly to water pollution because many of the chemicals and toxic wastes that are dumped on the land eventually work their way into the water supply. A study conducted by the Environmental Protection Agency found residues of prescription drugs, soaps, and other contaminants in virtually every waterway in the United States. Effects of these pollutants on humans and wildlife are uncertain, but there is some evidence to suggest that fish and other water-dwellers are starting to suffer serious effects.[58] Land pollution results from the dumping of residential and industrial waste, strip mining, forest fires, and poor forest conservation. In Brazil and other South American countries, rain forests are being destroyed—to make way for farms and ranches, at a cost of the extinction of the many animals and plants (some endangered species) that call the rain forest home. For example, annual deforestation in the Brazilian rainforest encompasses an area about the size of Delaware. The good news is that deforestation rates in Brazil may be decreasing due to new laws against illegal logging.[59] Large-scale deforestation also depletes the oxygen supply available to humans and other animals.

Related to the problem of land pollution is the larger issue of how to dispose of waste in an environmentally responsible manner. Americans discard nearly 7 million tons of plastic bags each year. Hawaii has banned plastic bag use, and California, Delaware, New York, Illinois, Maine, and Rhode Island have adopted reuse, relabel, or recycling programs for plastic bags.[60] Starting in 2014, Los Angeles also banned plastic bag use. Under the new law, shoppers will have to bring their own reusable bags or pay 10 cents for each paper bag. Los Angeles is the biggest city in the United States to ban plastic bag usage so far.[61]

替代能源

Alternative Energy. With ongoing plans to reduce global carbon emissions, countries and companies alike are looking toward alternative energy sources. Traditional

Solar power is growing in popularity as an alternative to traditional fuel sources, as this solar-power race car demonstrates.

fossil fuels are problematic because of their emissions, but also because stores have been greatly depleted. Foreign fossil fuels are often imported from politically and economically unstable regions, often making it unsafe to conduct business there. However, the United States is becoming an energy powerhouse with its ability to drill for natural gas in large shale reserves. This is allowing the United States to move forward on its goals to reach energy independence. On the other hand, concerns over how these drilling methods are affecting the environment make this a controversial topic.

With global warming concerns and rising gas prices, the U.S. government has begun to recognize the need to look toward alternative forms of energy as a source of fuel and electricity. There have been many different ideas as to which form of alternative energy would best suit the United States' energy needs. These sources include wind power, solar power, nuclear power, biofuels, electric cars, and hydro- and geothermal power. As of yet, no "best" form of alternative fuel has been selected to replace gasoline. Additionally, there are numerous challenges with the economic viability of alternative energy sources. For instance, wind and solar power cost significantly more than traditional energy; watts from wind power are estimated to be 290 percent higher than from natural gas, and the costs of solar photovoltaic is estimated to be 230 percent more expensive. Alternative energy will likely require government subsidies to make any significant strides. However, the news for solar power might be getting brighter. First Solar, an Arizona-based manufacturer of solar photovoltaic modules, has rebounded. Heavy competition from Chinese solar manufacturers had eaten up some of First Solar's profits and bankrupted other American solar companies. Yet First Solar's growth prospects appear to be high, reflected in their climbing stock price.[62]

对环境问题的回应

Response to Environmental Issues. Partly in response to federal legislation such as the National Environmental Policy Act of 1969 and partly due to consumer concerns, businesses are responding to environmental issues. Many small and large companies, including Walt Disney Company, Chevron, and Scott Paper, have created an executive position—a vice president of environmental affairs—to help them achieve their business goals in an environmentally responsible manner. Some companies are finding that environmental consciousness can save them money. For example, one San Diego hotel saved more than $40,000 by changing how it uses energy and adopting more energy-saving devices.[63]

Many firms are trying to eliminate wasteful practices, the emission of pollutants, and/or the use of harmful chemicals from their manufacturing processes. Other companies are seeking ways to improve their products. Utility providers, for example, are increasingly supplementing their services with alternative energy sources, including solar, wind, and geothermal power. Environmentalists are concerned that some companies are merely *greenwashing,* or "creating a positive association with environmental issues for an unsuitable product, service, or practice."

DID YOU KNOW? **Americans generate 4.4 million tons of electronic waste each year, including discarded laptops, mobile phones, and televisions.[64]**

In many places, local utility customers can even elect to purchase electricity from green sources—primarily wind power—for a few extra dollars a month. Austin Energy of Austin, Texas, has an award-winning GreenChoice program that includes many small and large businesses among its customers.[65] Indeed, a growing number of businesses and consumers are choosing green power sources where available. New Belgium Brewing Company, the third-largest craft brewer in the United States, is the first all-wind-powered brewery in the country. Many businesses have turned to *recycling,* the reprocessing of materials—aluminum, paper, glass, and some plastic—for reuse. Such efforts to make products, packaging, and processes more environmentally friendly have been labeled "green" business or marketing by the public and media. New Belgium, for instance, started selling aluminum cans of its beers because aluminum is easily recyclable and creates less waste. Lumber products at The Home Depot may carry a seal from the Forest Stewardship Council to indicate that they were harvested from sustainable forests using environmentally friendly methods.[66] Likewise, most Chiquita bananas are certified through the Better Banana Project as having been grown with more environmentally and labor-friendly practices.[67]

It is important to recognize that, with current technology, environmental responsibility requires trade-offs. Society must weigh the huge costs of limiting or eliminating pollution against the health threat posed by the pollution. Environmental responsibility imposes costs on both business and the public. Although people certainly do not want oil fouling beautiful waterways and killing wildlife, they insist on low-cost, readily available gasoline and heating oil. People do not want to contribute to the growing garbage-disposal problem, but they often refuse to pay more for "green" products packaged in an environmentally friendly manner, to recycle as much of their own waste as possible, or to permit the building of additional waste-disposal facilities (the "not in my backyard," or NIMBY, syndrome). Managers must coordinate environmental goals with other social and economic ones.

与社区的关系

Community Relations. A final, yet very significant, issue for businesses concerns their responsibilities to the general welfare of the communities and societies in which they operate. Many businesses simply want to make their communities better places for everyone to live and work. The most common way that businesses exercise their community responsibility is through donations to local and national charitable organizations. For example, General Electric employees hold fundraising efforts to raise money for the United Way. Additionally, GE donates 2 percent of its appliance sales from its online GE Appliance Outlet Store to the United Way.[68] Small businesses also give back to their communities. Chattanooga-based coffee retailer Blue Smoke Coffee donates 10 percent of its sales to environmental and humanitarian causes.[69] Even small companies participate in philanthropy through donations and volunteer support of local causes and national charities, such as the Red Cross and the United Way.

失业
Unemployment

After realizing that the current pool of prospective employees lacks many basic skills necessary to work, many companies have become concerned about the quality of education in the United States. Unemployment has become a significant problem since the onset of the financial crisis in 2008. In the years following, unemployment reached as high as 10 percent in the United States. Although it has fallen to about 7 percent since then, many consumers remain unemployed.[70]

Although most would argue that unemployment is an economic issue, it also carries ethical implications. Protests often occur in areas where unemployment is high, particularly when there seems to be a large gap between rich and poor. In Spain, high rates of unemployment caused unemployed citizens to arrange protests in the capital city of Madrid. Because Spain had received bailout money, international leaders have demanded steep spending cuts and tax rises. This has led to the unemployment of more than 6 million individuals. Spanish citizens protested the spending cuts imposed on them by other countries, feeling like they were unethical because they led to higher unemployment.[71]

Thousands of jobs were lost after Blockbuster shuttered its stores.

Factory closures are another ethical issue because factories usually employ hundreds of workers. Sometimes it is necessary to close a plant due to economic reasons. However, factory closures not only affect individual employees, but their communities as well. When an Electrolux factory moved from Webster City, Iowa, to Juarez, Mexico, the city of 8,000 people lost its main employer. This is having repercussions on other businesses in the area because more unemployed people mean fewer sales.[72]

Another criticism levied against companies involves hiring standards. Studies appear to show that while there are plenty of people unemployed, approximately 35 percent of companies cite employees' lack of experience as to why there are so many unfilled positions. Yet only about 28 percent are investing in more training and development for new hires. While it is important for employees to have certain skills, many feel that businesses must be willing to train employees if they want to fill their vacancies and decrease the unemployment rate.[73]

On the other hand, several businesses are working to reduce unemployment. After becoming frustrated with high unemployment rates, Starbucks founder and CEO Howard Schultz partnered with a national network of community lenders called Opportunity Network to develop Create Jobs for USA. This program provides funding for community businesses with the intent to reduce unemployment in their areas. Starbucks initially donated $5 million to the initiative. Other companies have also made significant contributions, including Banana Republic, Citi, Google Offers, and MasterCard.[74]

Additionally, businesses are beginning to take more responsibility for the hard-core unemployed. These are people who have never had a job or who have been unemployed for a long period of time. Some are mentally or physically handicapped; some are homeless. Organizations such as the National Alliance of Businessmen fund programs to train the hard-core unemployed so that they can find jobs and support themselves. Also, while numerous businesses laid off employees during the last recession, others were praised for their refusal to lay off workers. Boston Consulting Group (BCG), for instance, avoided laying off employees during the recession. As a result, employees at BCG are highly motivated and voted BCG as one of the best companies to work for.[75] Such commitment enhances self-esteem and helps people become productive members of society.

So You Want a Job in Business Ethics and Social Responsibility

In the words of Kermit the Frog, "It's not easy being green." It may not be easy, but green business opportunities abound. A popular catch phrase, "Green is the new black," indicates how fashionable green business is becoming. Consumers are more in tune with and concerned about green products, policies, and behaviors by companies than ever before. Companies are looking for new hires to help them see their business creatively and bring insights to all aspects of business operations. The American Solar Energy Society estimates that the number of green jobs could rise to 40 million in the United States by 2030. Green business strategies not only give a firm a commercial advantage in the marketplace, but help lead the way toward a greener world. The fight to reduce our carbon footprint in an attempt against climate change has opened up opportunities for renewable energy, recycling, conservation, and increasing overall efficiency in the way resources are used. New businesses that focus on hydro, wind, and solar power are on the rise and will need talented businesspeople to lead them. Carbon emissions' trading is gaining popularity as large corporations and individuals alike seek to lower their footprints. A job in this growing field could be similar to that of a stock trader, or you could lead the search for carbon-efficient companies in which to invest.

In the ethics arena, current trends in business governance strongly support the development of ethics and compliance departments to help guide organizational integrity. This alone is a billion-dollar business, and there are jobs in developing organizational ethics programs, developing company policies, and training employees and management. An entry-level position might be as a communication specialist or trainer for programs in a business ethics department. Eventually there's an opportunity to become an ethics officer that would have typical responsibilities of meeting with employees, the board of directors, and top management to discuss and provide advice about ethics issues in the industry, developing and distributing a code of ethics, creating and maintaining an anonymous, confidential service to answer questions about ethical issues, taking actions on possible ethics code violations, and reviewing and modifying the code of ethics of the organization.

There are also opportunities to help with initiatives to help companies relate social responsibility to stakeholder interests and needs. These jobs could involve coordinating and implementing philanthropic programs that give back to others important to the organization or developing a community volunteering program for employees. In addition to the human relations function, most companies develop programs to assist employees and their families to improve their quality of life. Companies have found that the healthier and happier employees are the more productive they will be in the workforce.

Social responsibility, ethics, and sustainable business practices are not a trend, they are good for business and the bottom line. New industries are being created and old ones are adapting to the new market demands, opening up many varied job opportunities that will lead not only to a paycheck, but also to the satisfaction of making the world a better place.[76]

Review Your Understanding

Define business ethics and social responsibility and examine their importance.

Business ethics refers to principles and standards that define acceptable business conduct. Acceptable business behavior is defined by customers, competitors, government regulators, interest groups, the public, and each individual's personal moral principles and values. Social responsibility is the obligation an organization assumes to maximize its positive impact and minimize its negative impact on society. Socially responsible businesses win the trust and respect of their employees, customers, and society and, in the long run, increase profits. Ethics is important in business because it builds trust and confidence in business relationships. Unethical actions may result in negative publicity, declining sales, and even legal action.

Detect some of the ethical issues that may arise in business.

An ethical issue is an identifiable problem, situation, or opportunity requiring a person or organization to choose from among several actions that must be evaluated as right or wrong. Ethical issues can be categorized in the context of their relation with conflicts of interest, fairness and honesty, communications, and business associations.

Specify how businesses can promote ethical behavior by employees.

Businesses can promote ethical behavior by employees by limiting their opportunity to engage in misconduct. Formal codes of ethics, ethical policies, and ethics training programs reduce the incidence of unethical behavior by informing employees what is expected of them and providing punishments for those who fail to comply.

Explain the four dimensions of social responsibility.

The four dimensions of social responsibility are economic or financial viability (being profitable), legal (obeying the law), ethical (doing what is right, just, and fair), and philanthropic, or voluntary (being a good corporate citizen).

Debate an organization's social responsibilities to owners, employees, consumers, the environment, and the community.

Businesses must maintain proper accounting procedures, provide all relevant information about the performance of the firm to investors, and protect the owners' rights and investments. In relations with employees, businesses are expected to provide a safe workplace, pay employees adequately for their work, and treat them fairly. Consumerism refers to the activities undertaken by independent individuals, groups, and organizations to protect their rights as consumers. Increasingly, society expects businesses to take greater responsibility for the environment, especially with regard to animal rights, as well as water, air, land, and noise pollution. Many businesses engage in activities to make the communities in which they operate better places for everyone to live and work.

Evaluate the ethics of a business's decision.

"Solve the Dilemma" on page 65 presents an ethical dilemma at Checkers Pizza. Using the material presented in this chapter, you should be able to analyze the ethical issues present in the dilemma, evaluate Barnard's plan, and develop a course of action for the firm.

Revisit the World of Business

1. Describe the ethical issue.
2. What are some of the potential negative effects of triclosan?
3. What impact could the FDA's proposal have on soap manufacturers?

Learn the Terms

bribes
business ethics
codes of ethics
consumerism
corporate citizenship
ethical issue
plagiarism
social responsibility
sustainability
whistleblowing

Check Your Progress

1. Define business ethics. Who determines whether a business activity is ethical? Is unethical conduct always illegal?
2. Distinguish between ethics and social responsibility.
3. Why has ethics become so important in business?
4. What is an ethical issue? What are some of the ethical issues named in your text? Why are they ethical issues?
5. What is a code of ethics? How can one reduce unethical behavior in business?
6. List and discuss the arguments for and against social responsibility by business (Table 2.9). Can you think of any additional arguments (for or against)?
7. What responsibilities does a business have toward its employees?
8. What responsibilities does business have with regard to the environment? What steps have been taken by some responsible businesses to minimize the negative impact of their activities on the environment?
9. What are a business's responsibilities toward the community in which it operates?

Get Involved

1. Discuss some recent examples of businesses engaging in unethical practices. Classify these practices as issues of conflict of interest, fairness and honesty, communications, or business relationships. Why do you think the businesses chose to behave unethically? What actions might the businesses have taken?
2. Discuss with your class some possible methods of improving ethical standards in business. Do you think that business should regulate its own activities or that the federal government should establish and enforce ethical standards? How do you think businesspeople feel?
3. Find some examples of socially responsible businesses in newspapers or business journals. Explain why you believe their actions are socially responsible. Why do you think the companies chose to act as they did?

Build Your Skills

Making Decisions about Ethical Issues

Background

The merger of Lockheed and Martin Marietta created Lockheed Martin, the number-one company in the defense industry—an industry that includes such companies as Raytheon and Northrop Grumman.

You and the rest of the class are managers at Lockheed Martin Corporation, Orlando, Florida. You are getting ready to do the group exercise in an ethics training session. The training instructor announces you will be playing *Gray Matters: The Ethics Game*. You are told that *Gray Matters,* which was prepared for your company's employees, is also played at 41 universities, including Harvard University, and at 65 other companies. Although there are 55 scenarios in *Gray Matters,* you will have time during this session to complete only the four scenarios that your group draws from the stack of cards.[77]

Task

Form into groups of four to six managers and appoint a group leader who will lead a discussion of the case, obtain a consensus answer to the case, and be the one to report the group's answers to the instructor. You will have five minutes to reach each decision, after which time, the instructor will give the point values and rationale for each choice. Then you will have five minutes for the next case, etc., until all four cases have been completed. Keep track of your group's score for each case; the winning team will be the group scoring the most points.

Since this game is designed to reflect life, you may believe that some cases lack clarity or that some of your choices are not as precise as you would have liked. Also, some cases have only one solution, while others have more than one solution. Each choice is assessed to reflect which answer is the most correct. **Your group's task is to select only one option in each case.**

4

Mini-Case

For several months now, one of your colleagues has been slacking off, and you are getting stuck doing the work. You think it is unfair. What do you do?

Potential Answers

A. Recognize this as an opportunity for you to demonstrate how capable you are.
B. Go to your supervisor and complain about this unfair workload.
C. Discuss the problem with your colleague in an attempt to solve the problem without involving others.
D. Discuss the problem with the human resources department.

7

Mini-Case

You are aware that a fellow employee uses drugs on the job. Another friend encourages you to confront the person instead of informing the supervisor. What do you do?

Potential Answers

A. You speak to the alleged user and encourage him to get help.
B. You elect to tell your supervisor that you suspect an employee is using drugs on the job.
C. You confront the alleged user and tell him either to quit using drugs or you will "turn him in."
D. Report the matter to employee assistance.

36

Mini-Case

You work for a company that has implemented a policy of a smoke-free environment. You discover employees smoking in the restrooms of the building. You also smoke and don't like having to go outside to do it. What do you do?

Potential Answers

A. You ignore the situation.
B. You confront the employees and ask them to stop.
C. You join them, but only occasionally.
D. You contact your ethics or human resources representative and ask him or her to handle the situation.

40

Mini-Case

Your co-worker is copying company-purchased software and taking it home. You know a certain program costs $400, and you have been saving for a while to buy it. What do you do?

Potential Answers

A. You figure you can copy it too since nothing has ever happened to your co-worker.
B. You tell your co-worker he can't legally do this.
C. You report the matter to the ethics office.
D. You mention this to your supervisor.

Solve the Dilemma

LO 2-6

Customer Privacy

Checkers Pizza was one of the first to offer home delivery service, with overwhelming success. However, the major pizza chains soon followed suit, taking away Checkers's competitive edge. Jon Barnard, Checkers's founder and co-owner, needed a new gimmick to beat the competition. He decided to develop a computerized information database that would make Checkers the most efficient competitor and provide insight into consumer buying behavior at the same time. Under the system, telephone customers were asked their phone number; if they had ordered from Checkers before, their address and previous order information came up on the computer screen.

After successfully testing the new system, Barnard put the computerized order network in place in all Checkers outlets. After three months of success, he decided to give an award to the family that ate the most Checkers pizza. Through the tracking system, the company identified the biggest customer, who had ordered a pizza every weekday for the past three months (63 pizzas). The company put together a program to surprise the family with an award, free-food certificates, and a news story announcing the award. As Barnard began to plan for the event, however, he began to think that maybe the family might not want all the attention and publicity.

Discussion Questions

1. What are some of the ethical issues in giving customers an award for consumption behavior without notifying them first?
2. Do you see this as a potential violation of privacy? Explain.
3. How would you handle the situation if you were Barnard?

Build Your Business Plan

Business Ethics and Social Responsibility

Think about which industry you are considering competing in with your good/service. Is there any kind of questionable practices in the way the product has been traditionally sold? Produced? Advertised? Have there been any recent accusations regarding safety within the industry? What about any environmental concerns?

For example, if you are thinking of opening a lawn care business, you need to be thinking about what possible effects the chemicals you are using will have on the client and the environment. You have a responsibility to keep your customers safe and healthy. You also have the social responsibility to let the community know of any damaging effect you may be directly or indirectly responsible for.

See for Yourself Videocase

The Challenge of Building Trust in Business

Corporate scandals, a growing awareness of environmental issues, and the last global recession have greatly altered the public's perspective of corporate America. Gone are the days in which consumers blindly trusted company publicity and rhetoric. The public's trust in business has been shattered, and many companies have a long way to go to earn it back.

The Arthur Page Society and the Business Roundtable Institute for Corporate Ethics are dedicated to corporate accountability and ethics. The organizations released a study addressing Americans' mistrust of business and how corporations can begin to win back the hearts and minds of consumers. The study, entitled "The Dynamics of Public Trust in Business—Emerging Opportunities for Leaders," shows that public trust in business has reached a low point. As the economy begins to recover, trust in business has increased. However, trust of business continues to be a serious challenge for businesses to overcome. This presents major difficulties for businesses because trust is the glue that holds relationships together.

A major issue appears to be the imbalance of power. Many consumers are still angry over business scandals and unemployment rates while corporate management still makes huge profits. The government defended corporate bailouts as a way to keep large companies from failing (which could have worsened the recession). Most of the money has since been paid back, and the government has made a profit. Unemployment has decreased in the last few years, although among young people it is still 15 percent. It is believed that if youth unemployment returned to pre-recession rates, the federal government would recoup $7.8 billion.

Distrust of business is not limited to the United States. According to the Edelman Trust Barometer, 54 percent of global consumers indicate that they trust business. Financial service institutions and banks have the lowest rankings in consumer trust worldwide, at 51 percent. More recent scandals at J.P. Morgan Stanley, HSBC, and British financial services firm Barclays continue to keep trust in this sector low.

Although the Arthur Page Society and the Business Roundtable see their report as a way to start a national dialogue, the report does offer a series of suggestions for businesses. First and foremost, the balance of power must be equalized. Companies must focus on creating mutual value and leaders must try to gain and retain trust. The study also suggests that corporations create quality goods/services, sell goods/services at fair prices, create and maintain positive employment practices, give investors a fair return, remain active in social responsibility, and create transparency.

Most firms have not been involved in scandals or misconduct. In fact, most companies operate in an ethical and socially responsible manner. Unfortunately, the public sees reports of misconduct in a few businesses and generalizes the misconduct to all businesses. Nevertheless, companies need to communicate their values and maintain responsible conduct. Another example involves the growing public concern regarding how businesses affect the environment—investors want details on a business's impact and what that business is doing to be more sustainable. As the public fights to make its desires known regarding business behavior, businesses that sincerely want to help the world are receiving some help. Maryland, Vermont, New York, California, and three other states have made "benefit corporations" legal. These corporations must make their values public, report yearly on their socially beneficial behavior, and agree to third-party audits of their social responsibility actions. Acquiring this designation requires the approval of more than half a company's shareholders. Companies may also establish themselves as B corporations, which certifies their socially responsible focus. It is entirely possible for businesses to regain public trust, but it means a change in values for many businesses in today's corporate America.[78]

Discussion Questions

1. What are some of the reasons cited in the Arthur Page Society and the Business Roundtable Institute for Corporate Ethics report for public distrust of corporations?
2. What are some of the recommendations made by the report? Can you think of any other recommendations to give companies on how to behave more ethically?
3. What are the benefits of being perceived as an ethical company? What are the downsides of having a reputation for ethical misconduct?

You can find the related video in the Video Library in Connect. Ask your instructor how you can access Connect.

Team Exercise

Sam Walton, founder of Walmart, had an early strategy for growing his business related to pricing. The "Opening Price Point" strategy used by Walton involved offering the introductory product in a product line at the lowest point in the market. For example, a minimally equipped microwave oven would sell for less than anyone else in town could sell the same unit. The strategy was that if consumers saw a product, such as the microwave, and saw it as a good value, they would assume that all of the microwaves were good values. Walton also noted that most people don't buy the entry-level product; they want more features and capabilities and often trade up.

Form teams and assign the role of defending this strategy or casting this strategy as an unethical act. Present your thoughts on either side of the issue.

附录 B

法律与监管环境
The Legal and Regulatory Environment

Business law refers to the rules and regulations that govern the conduct of business. Problems in this area come from the failure to keep promises, misunderstandings, disagreements about expectations, or, in some cases, attempts to take advantage of others. The regulatory environment offers a framework and enforcement system in order to provide a fair playing field for all businesses. The regulatory environment is created based on inputs from competitors, customers, employees, special interest groups, and the public's elected representatives. Lobbying by pressure groups who try to influence legislation often shapes the legal and regulatory environment.

法律渊源
Sources of Law

Laws are classified as either criminal or civil. *Criminal law* not only prohibits a specific kind of action, such as unfair competition or mail fraud, but also imposes a fine or imprisonment as punishment for violating the law. A violation of a criminal law is thus called a crime. *Civil law* defines all the laws not classified as criminal, and it specifies the rights and duties of individuals and organizations (including businesses). Violations of civil law may result in fines but not imprisonment. The primary difference between criminal and civil law is that criminal laws are enforced by the state or nation, whereas civil laws are enforced through the court system by individuals or organizations.

Criminal and civil laws are derived from four sources: the Constitution (constitutional law), precedents established by judges (common law), federal and state statutes (statutory law), and federal and state administrative agencies (administrative law). Federal administrative agencies established by Congress control and influence business by enforcing laws and regulations to encourage competition and protect consumers, workers, and the environment. The Supreme Court is the ultimate authority on legal and regulatory decisions for appropriate conduct in business.

法院与纠纷解决
Courts and the Resolution of Disputes

The primary method of resolving conflicts and business disputes is through **lawsuits,** where one individual or organization takes another to court using civil laws. The legal system, therefore, provides a forum for businesspeople to resolve disputes based on our legal foundations. The courts may decide when harm or damage results from the actions of others.

Because lawsuits are so frequent in the world of business, it is important to understand more about the court system where such disputes are resolved. Both financial restitution and specific actions to undo wrongdoing can result from going before a court to resolve a conflict. All decisions made in the courts are based on criminal and civil laws derived from the legal and regulatory system.

A businessperson may win a lawsuit in court and receive a judgment, or court order, requiring the loser of the suit to pay monetary damages. However, this does not guarantee the victor will be able to collect those damages. If the loser of the suit lacks the financial

Hostess workers went on strike to protest wages. The company responded by declaring bankrupcty. Although a judge ordered mediation between Hostess and the union, an agreement was not reached and Hostess closed down.

resources to pay the judgment—for example, if the loser is a bankrupt business—the winner of the suit may not be able to collect the award. Most business lawsuits involve a request for a sum of money, but some lawsuits request that a court specifically order a person or organization to do or to refrain from doing a certain act, such as slamming telephone customers.

法院系统 The Court System

Jurisdiction is the legal power of a court, through a judge, to interpret and apply the law and make a binding decision in a particular case. In some instances, other courts will not enforce the decision of a prior court because it lacked jurisdiction. Federal courts are granted jurisdiction by the Constitution or by Congress. State legislatures and constitutions determine which state courts hear certain types of cases. Courts of general jurisdiction hear all types of cases; those of limited jurisdiction hear only specific types of cases. The Federal Bankruptcy Court, for example, hears only cases involving bankruptcy. There is some combination of limited and general jurisdiction courts in every state.

In a **trial court** (whether in a court of general or limited jurisdiction and whether in the state or the federal system), two tasks must be completed. First, the court (acting through the judge or a jury) must determine the facts of the case. In other words, if there is conflicting evidence, the judge or jury must decide who to believe. Second, the judge must decide which law or set of laws is pertinent to the case and must then apply those laws to resolve the dispute.

An **appellate court,** on the other hand, deals solely with appeals relating to the interpretation of law. Thus, when you hear about a case being appealed, it is not retried, but rather reevaluated. Appellate judges do not hear witnesses but instead base their decisions on a written transcript of the original trial. Moreover, appellate courts do not draw factual conclusions; the appellate judge is limited to deciding whether the trial judge made a mistake in interpreting the law that probably affected the outcome of the trial. If the trial judge made no mistake (or if mistakes would not have changed the result of the trial), the appellate court will let the trial court's decision stand. If the appellate court finds a mistake, it usually sends the case back to the trial court so that the mistake can be corrected. Correction may involve the granting of a new trial. On occasion, appellate courts modify the verdict of the trial court without sending the case back to the trial court.

解决争端的其他方法 Alternative Dispute Resolution Methods

Although the main remedy for business disputes is a lawsuit, other dispute resolution methods are becoming popular. The schedules of state and federal trial courts are often crowded; long delays between the filing of a case and the trial date are common. Further, complex cases can become quite expensive to pursue. As a result, many businesspeople are turning to alternative methods of resolving business arguments: mediation and arbitration, the mini-trial, and litigation in a private court.

Mediation is a form of negotiation to resolve a dispute by bringing in one or more third-party mediators, usually chosen by the disputing parties, to help reach a settlement. The mediator suggests different ways to resolve a dispute between the parties. The mediator's resolution is nonbinding—that is, the parties do not have to accept the mediator's suggestions; they are strictly voluntary.

Arbitration involves submission of a dispute to one or more third-party arbitrators, usually chosen by the disputing parties, whose decision usually is final. Arbitration differs from mediation in that an arbitrator's decision must be followed, whereas a mediator merely offers suggestions and facilitates negotiations. Cases may be submitted to arbitration because a contract—such as a labor contract—requires it or because the parties agree to do so. Some consumers are barred from taking claims to court by agreements drafted by banks, brokers, health plans, and others. Instead, they are required to take complaints to mandatory arbitration. Arbitration can be an attractive alternative to a lawsuit because it is often cheaper and quicker, and the parties frequently can choose arbitrators who are knowledgeable about the particular area of business at issue.

A method of dispute resolution that may become increasingly important in settling complex disputes is the **mini-trial,** in which both parties agree to present a summarized version of their case to an independent third party. That person then advises them of his or her impression of the probable outcome if the case were to be tried. Representatives of both sides then attempt to negotiate a settlement based on the advisor's recommendations. For example, employees in a large corporation who believe they have muscular or skeletal stress injuries caused by the strain of repetitive motion in using a computer could agree to a mini-trial to address a dispute related to damages. Although the mini-trial itself does not resolve the dispute, it can help the parties resolve the case before going to court. Because the mini-trial is not subject to formal court rules, it can save companies a great deal of money, allowing them to recognize the weaknesses in a particular case.

In some areas of the country, disputes can be submitted to a private nongovernmental court for resolution. In a sense, a **private court system** is similar to arbitration in that an independent third party resolves the case after hearing both sides of the story. Trials in private courts may be either informal or highly formal, depending on the people involved. Businesses typically agree to have their disputes decided in private courts to save time and money.

监管行政机构
Regulatory Administrative Agencies

Federal and state administrative agencies (listed in Table B.1) also have some judicial powers. Many administrative agencies, such as the Federal Trade Commission, decide disputes that involve their regulations. In such disputes, the resolution process is usually called a "hearing" rather than a trial. In these cases, an administrative law judge decides all issues.

Federal regulatory agencies influence many business activities and cover product liability, safety, and

TABLE B.1 The Major Regulatory Agencies

Agency	Major Areas of Responsibility
Federal Trade Commission (FTC)	Enforces laws and guidelines regarding business practices; takes action to stop false and deceptive advertising and labeling.
Food and Drug Administration (FDA)	Enforces laws and regulations to prevent distribution of adulterated or misbranded foods, drugs, medical devices, cosmetics, veterinary products, and particularly hazardous consumer products.
Consumer Product Safety Commission (CPSC)	Ensures compliance with the Consumer Product Safety Act; protects the public from unreasonable risk of injury from any consumer product not covered by other regulatory agencies.
Interstate Commerce Commission (ICC)	Regulates franchises, rates, and finances of interstate rail, bus, truck, and water carriers.
Federal Communications Commission (FCC)	Regulates communication by wire, radio, and television in interstate and foreign commerce.
Environmental Protection Agency (EPA)	Develops and enforces environmental protection standards and conducts research into the adverse effects of pollution.
Federal Energy Regulatory Commission (FERC)	Regulates rates and sales of natural gas products, thereby affecting the supply and price of gas available to consumers; also regulates wholesale rates for electricity and gas, pipeline construction, and U.S. imports and exports of natural gas and electricity.
Equal Employment Opportunity Commission (EEOC)	Investigates and resolves discrimination in employment practices.
Federal Aviation Administration (FAA)	Oversees the policies and regulations of the airline industry.
Federal Highway Administration (FHA)	Regulates vehicle safety requirements.
Occupational Safety and Health Administration (OSHA)	Develops policy to promote worker safety and health and investigates infractions.
Securities and Exchange Commission (SEC)	Regulates corporate securities trading and develops protection from fraud and other abuses; provides an accounting oversight board.

the regulation or deregulation of public utilities. Usually, these bodies have the power to enforce specific laws, such as the Federal Trade Commission Act, and have some discretion in establishing operating rules and regulations to guide certain types of industry practices. Because of this discretion and overlapping areas of responsibility, confusion or conflict regarding which agencies have jurisdiction over which activities is common.

Of all the federal regulatory units, the **Federal Trade Commission (FTC)** most influences business activities related to questionable practices that create disputes between businesses and their customers. Although the FTC regulates a variety of business practices, it allocates a large portion of resources to curbing false advertising, misleading pricing, and deceptive packaging and labeling. When it receives a complaint or otherwise has reason to believe that a firm is violating a law, the FTC issues a complaint stating that the business is in violation.

If a company continues the questionable practice, the FTC can issue a cease-and-desist order, which is an order for the business to stop doing whatever has caused the complaint. In such cases, the charged firm can appeal to the federal courts to have the order rescinded. However, the FTC can seek civil penalties in court—up to a maximum penalty of $10,000 a day for each infraction—if a cease-and-desist order is violated. In its battle against unfair pricing, the FTC has issued consent decrees alleging that corporate attempts to engage in price fixing or invitations to competitors to collude are violations even when the competitors in question refuse the invitations. The commission can also require companies to run corrective advertising in response to previous ads considered misleading.

The FTC also assists businesses in complying with laws. New marketing methods are evaluated every year. When general sets of guidelines are needed to improve business practices in a particular industry, the FTC sometimes encourages firms within that industry to establish a set of trade practices voluntarily. The FTC may even sponsor a conference bringing together industry leaders and consumers for the purpose of establishing acceptable trade practices.

Unlike the FTC, other regulatory units are limited to dealing with specific goods, services, or business activities. The Food and Drug Administration (FDA) enforces regulations prohibiting the sale and distribution of adulterated, misbranded, or hazardous food and drug products. For example, the FDA outlawed the sale and distribution of most over-the-counter hair-loss remedies after research indicated that few of the products were effective in restoring hair growth.

The Environmental Protection Agency (EPA) develops and enforces environmental protection standards and conducts research into the adverse effects of pollution. The Consumer Product Safety Commission recalls about 300 products a year, ranging from small, inexpensive toys to major appliances. The Consumer Product Safety Commission's website provides details regarding current recalls.

The Consumer Product Safety commission has fallen under increasing scrutiny in the wake of a number of product safety scandals involving children's toys. The most notable of these issues was lead paint discovered in some toys. Other problems have included the manufacture of toys that include small magnets that pose a choking hazard, and leadtainted costume jewelry.[79]

商法的重要元素
Important Elements of Business Law

To avoid violating criminal and civil laws, as well as discouraging lawsuits from consumers, employees, suppliers, and others, businesspeople need to be familiar with laws that address business practices.

美国统一商法典
The Uniform Commercial Code

At one time, states had their own specific laws governing various business practices, and transacting business across state lines was difficult because of the variation in the laws from state to state. To simplify commerce, every state—except Louisiana—has enacted the Uniform Commercial Code (Louisiana has enacted portions of the code). The **Uniform Commercial Code (UCC)** is a set of statutory laws covering several business law topics. Article II of the Uniform Commercial Code, which is discussed in the following paragraphs, has a significant impact on business.

销售协议

Sales Agreements. Article II of the Uniform Commercial Code covers sales agreements for goods and services such as installation but does not cover the sale of stocks and bonds, personal services, or real estate. Among its many provisions, Article II stipulates that a sales agreement can be enforced even though it does not specify the selling price or the time or place of delivery. It also requires that a buyer pay a reasonable price for goods at the time of delivery if the buyer and seller have not reached an agreement on price. Specifically, Article II addresses the rights of buyers and sellers, transfers of ownership, warranties, and the legal placement of risk during manufacture and delivery.

Article II also deals with express and implied warranties. An **express warranty** stipulates the specific terms the seller will honor. Many automobile manufacturers, for example, provide three-year or 36,000-mile warranties on their vehicles, during which period they will fix any and all defects specified in the warranty. An **implied warranty** is imposed on the producer or seller by law, although it may not be a written document provided at the time of sale. Under Article II, a consumer may assume that the product for sale has a clear title (in other words, that it is not stolen) and that the product will serve the purpose for which it was made and sold as well as function as advertised.

侵权法和欺诈法
The Law of Torts and Fraud

A **tort** is a private or civil wrong other than breach of contract. For example, a tort can result if the driver of a Domino's Pizza delivery car loses control of the vehicle and damages property or injures a person. In the case of the delivery car accident, the injured persons might sue the driver and the owner of the company—Domino's in this case—for damages resulting from the accident.

Fraud is a purposefully unlawful act to deceive or manipulate in order to damage others. Thus, in some cases, a tort may also represent a violation of criminal law. Health care fraud has become a major issue in the courts.

An important aspect of tort law involves **product liability**—businesses' legal responsibility for any negligence in the design, production, sale, and consumption of products. Product liability laws have evolved from both common and statutory law. Some states have expanded the concept of product liability to include injuries by products whether or not the producer is proven negligent. Under this strict product liability, a consumer who files suit because of an injury has to prove only that the product was defective, that the defect caused the injury, and that the defect made the product unreasonably dangerous. For example, a carving knife is expected to be sharp and is not considered defective if you cut your finger using it. But an electric knife could be considered defective and unreasonably dangerous if it continued to operate after being switched off.

Reforming tort law, particularly in regard to product liability, has become a hot political issue as businesses look for relief from huge judgments in lawsuits. Although many lawsuits are warranted—few would disagree that a wrong has occurred when a patient dies because of negligence during a medical procedure or when a child is seriously injured by a defective toy, and that the families deserve some compensation—many suits are not. Because of multimillion-dollar judgments, companies are trying to minimize their liability, and sometimes they pass on the costs of the damage awards to their customers in the form of higher prices. Some states have passed laws limiting damage awards and some tort reform is occurring at the federal level. Table B.2 lists the state courts systems the U.S. Chamber of Commerce's Institute for Legal Reform has identified as being "friendliest" and "least friendly" to business in terms

TABLE B.2 State Court Systems' Reputations for Supporting Business

Most Friendly to Business	Least Friendly to Business
Delaware	West Virginia
Nebraska	Louisiana
Wyoming	Mississippi
Minnesota	California
Kansas	Illinois
Idaho	Montana
Virginia	New Mexico
North Dakota	Alabama
Utah	Oklahoma
Iowa	Florida

Source: U.S. Chamber Institute for Legal Reform, "States".

of juries' fairness, judges' competence and impartiality, and other factors.

合同法
The Law of Contracts

Virtually every business transaction is carried out by means of a **contract,** a mutual agreement between two or more parties that can be enforced in a court if one party chooses not to comply with the terms of the contract. If you rent an apartment or house, for example, your lease is a contract. If you have borrowed money under a student loan program, you have a contractual agreement to repay the money. Many aspects of contract law are covered under the Uniform Commercial Code.

A "handshake deal" is in most cases as fully and completely binding as a written, signed contract agreement. Indeed, many oil-drilling and construction contractors have for years agreed to take on projects on the basis of such handshake deals. However, individual states require that some contracts be in writing to be enforceable. Most states require that at least some of the following contracts be in writing:

- Contracts involving the sale of land or an interest in land
- Contracts to pay somebody else's debt
- Contracts that cannot be fulfilled within one year
- Contracts for the sale of goods that cost more than $500 (required by the Uniform Commercial Code)

Only those contracts that meet certain requirements—called *elements*—are enforceable by the courts. A person or business seeking to enforce a contract must show that it contains the following elements: voluntary agreement, consideration, contractual capacity of the parties, and legality.

For any agreement to be considered a legal contract, all persons involved must agree to be bound by the terms of the contract. *Voluntary agreement* typically comes about when one party makes an offer and the other accepts. If both the offer and the acceptance are freely, voluntarily, and knowingly made, the acceptance forms the basis for the contract. If, however, either the offer or the acceptance is the result of fraud or force, the individual or organization subject to the fraud or force can void, or invalidate, the resulting agreement or receive compensation for damages.

The second requirement for enforcement of a contract is that it must be supported by *consideration*—that is, money or something of value must be given in return for fulfilling a contract. As a general rule, a person cannot be forced to abide by the terms of a promise unless that person receives a consideration. The something of value could be money, goods, services, or even a promise to do or not to do something.

Contractual capacity is the legal ability to enter into a contract. As a general rule, a court cannot enforce a contract if either party to the agreement lacks contractual capacity. A person's contractual capacity may be limited or nonexistent if he or she is a minor (under the age of 18), mentally unstable, retarded, insane, or intoxicated.

Legality is the state or condition of being lawful. For an otherwise binding contract to be enforceable, both the purpose of and the consideration for the contract must be legal. A contract in which a bank loans money at a rate of interest prohibited by law, a practice known as usury, would be an illegal contract, for example. The fact that one of the parties may commit an illegal act while performing a contract does not render the contract itself illegal, however.

Breach of contract is the failure or refusal of a party to a contract to live up to his or her promises. In the case of an apartment lease, failure to pay rent would be considered breach of contract. The breaching party—the one who fails to comply—may be liable for monetary damages that he or she causes the other person.

代理法
The Law of Agency

An **agency** is a common business relationship created when one person acts on behalf of another and under that person's control. Two parties are involved in an agency relationship: The **principal** is the one who wishes to have a specific task accomplished; the **agent** is the one who acts on behalf of the principal to accomplish the task. Authors, movie stars, and athletes often employ agents to help them obtain the best contract terms.

An agency relationship is created by the mutual agreement of the principal and the agent. It is usually not necessary that such an agreement be in writing, although putting it in writing is certainly advisable. An agency relationship continues as long as both the principal and the agent so desire. It can be terminated by mutual agreement, by fulfillment of the purpose of the agency, by the refusal of either party to continue in the relationship, or by the death of either the principal or the agent. In most cases, a principal grants authority to the agent through a formal *power of attorney,* which is a legal document authorizing a person to act as someone else's agent. The power of attorney can be used for any agency relationship, and its use is not limited to lawyers. For instance, in real estate transactions, often a lawyer or real estate agent is given power of attorney with the authority to purchase real estate for the buyer. Accounting firms often give employees agency relationships in making financial transactions.

Both officers and directors of corporations are fiduciaries, or people of trust, who use due care and loyalty as an agent in making decisions on behalf of the organization. This relationship creates a duty of care, also called duty of diligence, to make informed decisions. These agents of the corporation are not held responsible for negative outcomes if they are informed and diligent in their decisions. The duty of loyalty means that all decisions should be in the interests of the corporation and its stakeholders. Many people believe that executives at financial firms such as Countrywide Financial, Lehman Brothers, and Merrill Lynch failed to carry out their fiduciary duties. Lawsuits from shareholders called for the officers and directors to pay large sums of money from their own pockets.

物权法
The Law of Property

Property law is extremely broad in scope because it covers the ownership and transfer of all kinds of real, personal, and intellectual property. **Real property** consists of real estate and everything permanently attached to it; **personal property** basically is everything else. Personal property can be further subdivided into tangible and intangible property. *Tangible property* refers to items that have a physical existence, such as automobiles, business inventory, and clothing. *Intangible property* consists of rights and duties; its existence may be represented by a document or by some other tangible item. For example, accounts receivable, stock in a corporation, goodwill, and trademarks are all examples of intangible personal property. **Intellectual property** refers to property, such as musical works, artwork, books, and computer software, that is generated by a person's creative activities.

Copyrights, patents, and trademarks provide protection to the owners of property by giving them the exclusive right to use it. *Copyrights* protect the ownership rights on material (often intellectual property) such as books, music, videos, photos, and computer software. The creators of such works, or their heirs, generally have exclusive rights to the published or unpublished works for the creator's lifetime, plus 50 years. *Patents* give inventors exclusive rights to their invention for 20 years. The most intense competition for patents is in the pharmaceutical industry. Most patents take a minimum of 18 months to secure.

A *trademark* is a brand (name, mark, or symbol) that is registered with the U.S. Patent and Trademark Office and is thus legally protected from use by any other firm. Among the symbols that have been so protected are McDonald's golden arches and Coca-Cola's distinctive bottle shape. It is estimated that large multinational firms may have as many as 15,000 conflicts related to trademarks. Companies are diligent about protecting their trademarks both to avoid confusion in consumers' minds and because a term that becomes part of everyday language can no longer be trademarked. The names *aspirin* and *nylon,* for example, were once the exclusive property of their creators but became so widely used as product names (rather than brand names) that now anyone can use them.

As the trend toward globalization of trade continues, and more and more businesses trade across national boundaries, protecting property rights, particularly intellectual property such as computer software, has become an increasing challenge. While a company may be able to register as a trademark, a brand name, or a symbol in its home country, it may not be able to secure that protection abroad. Some countries have copyright and patent laws that are less strict than those of the United States; some countries will not enforce U.S. laws. Such counterfeiting harms not only the sales of U.S. companies but also their reputations if the knockoffs are of poor quality. Thus, businesses engaging in foreign trade may have to take extra steps to protect their property because local laws may be insufficient to protect them.

破产法
The Law of Bankruptcy

Although few businesses and individuals intentionally fail to repay (or default on) their debts, sometimes they cannot fulfill their financial obligations. Individuals may charge goods and services beyond their ability to pay for them. Businesses may take on too much debt in order to finance growth, or business events such as an increase in the cost of commodities can bankrupt a company. An option of last resort in these cases is bankruptcy, or legal insolvency. Some well-known companies that have declared bankruptcy include Hostess, American Airlines, and Blockbuster.

Individuals or companies may ask a bankruptcy court to declare them unable to pay their debts and thus release them from the obligation of repaying those debts. The debtor's assets may then be sold to pay off as much of the debt as possible. In the case of a personal bankruptcy, although the individual is released from repaying debts and can start over with a clean slate, obtaining credit after bankruptcy proceedings is very difficult. About 2 million households in the United States filed for bankruptcy in 2005, the most ever. However, a new, more restrictive law went into effect in late 2005, allowing fewer consumers to use bankruptcy to eliminate their debts. The law makes it harder for consumers to prove that they should be allowed to clear their debts for what is called a "fresh start" or bankruptcy. Although the person or company in debt usually initiates bankruptcy proceedings, creditors may also initiate them. The subprime mortgage crisis caused a string of bankruptcies among individuals, and bankruptcies among banks and other businesses as well. Tougher bankruptcy laws and a slowing economy converged on the subprime crisis to create a situation in which bankruptcy filings skyrocketed.

影响商业惯例的法律
Laws Affecting Business Practices

One of the government's many roles is to act as a watchdog to ensure that businesses behave in accordance with the wishes of society. Congress has enacted a number of laws that affect business practices; some of the most important of these are summarized in Table B.3. Many state legislatures have enacted similar laws governing business within specific states.

The **Sherman Antitrust Act,** passed in 1890 to prevent businesses from restraining trade and monopolizing markets, condemns "every contract, combination, or conspiracy in restraint of trade." For example, a request that a competitor agree to fix prices or divide markets would, if accepted, result in a violation of the Sherman Antitrust Act. American Airlines faced serious resistance from the U.S. Justice Department in its bid to acquire U.S. Airways. Because there are few major airlines in the United States, the Justice Department felt the merger could threaten competition and result in higher prices for consumers. The merger was eventually given the go-ahead after American Airlines agreed to give up some of its slots at major airports.[80] The Sherman Antitrust Act, still highly relevant 100 years after its passage, is being copied throughout the world as the basis for regulating fair competition.

Because the provisions of the Sherman Antitrust Act are rather vague, courts have not always interpreted it as its creators intended. The Clayton Act was passed in 1914 to limit specific activities that can reduce competition. The **Clayton Act** prohibits price discrimination, tying and exclusive agreements, and the acquisition of stock in another corporation where the effect may be to substantially lessen competition or tend to create a monopoly. In addition, the Clayton Act prohibits members of one company's board of directors from holding seats

TABLE B.3 Major Federal Laws Affecting Business Practices

Act (Date Enacted)	Purpose
Sherman Antitrust Act (1890)	Prohibits contracts, combinations, or conspiracies to restrain trade; establishes as a misdemeanor monopolizing or attempting to monopolize.
Clayton Act (1914)	Prohibits specific practices such as price discrimination, exclusive dealer arrangements, and stock acquisitions in which the effect may notably lessen competition or tend to create a monopoly.
Federal Trade Commission Act (1914)	Created the Federal Trade Commission; also gives the FTC investigatory powers to be used in preventing unfair methods of competition.
Robinson-Patman Act (1936)	Prohibits price discrimination that lessens competition among wholesalers or retailers; prohibits producers from giving disproportionate services of facilities to large buyers.
Wheeler-Lea Act (1938)	Prohibits unfair and deceptive acts and practices regardless of whether competition is injured; places advertising of foods and drugs under the jurisdiction of the FTC.
Lanham Act (1946)	Provides protections and regulation of brand names, brand marks, trade names, and trademarks.
Celler-Kefauver Act (1950)	Prohibits any corporation engaged in commerce from acquiring the whole or any part of the stock or other share of the capital assets of another corporation when the effect substantially lessens competition or tends to create a monopoly.
Fair Packaging and Labeling Act (1966)	Makes illegal the unfair or deceptive packaging or labeling of consumer products.
Magnuson-Moss Warranty (FTC) Act (1975)	Provides for minimum disclosure standards for written consumer product warranties; defines minimum consent standards for written warranties; allows the FTC to prescribe interpretive rules in policy statements regarding unfair or deceptive practices.
Consumer Goods Pricing Act (1975)	Prohibits the use of price maintenance agreements among manufacturers and resellers in interstate commerce.
Antitrust Improvements Act (1976)	Requires large corporations to inform federal regulators of prospective mergers or acquisitions so that they can be studied for any possible violations of the law.
Trademark Counterfeiting Act (1980)	Provides civil and criminal penalties against those who deal in counterfeit consumer goods or any counterfeit goods that can threaten health or safety.
Trademark Law Revision Act (1988)	Amends the Lanham Act to allow brands not yet introduced to be protected through registration with the Patent and Trademark Office.
Nutrition Labeling and Education Act (1990)	Prohibits exaggerated health claims and requires all processed foods to contain labels with nutritional information.
Telephone Consumer Protection Act (1991)	Establishes procedures to avoid unwanted telephone solicitations; prohibits marketers from using automated telephone dialing system or an artificial or prerecorded voice to certain telephone lines.
Federal Trademark Dilution Act (1995)	Provides trademark owners the right to protect trademarks and requires relinquishment of names that match or parallel existing trademarks.
Digital Millennium Copyright Act (1998)	Refined copyright laws to protect digital versions of copyrighted materials, including music and movies.

continued

TABLE B.3 continued

Act (Date Enacted)	Purpose
Children's Online Privacy Protection Act (2000)	Regulates the collection of personally identifiable information (name, address, e-mail address, hobbies, interests, or information collected through cookies) online from children under age 13.
Sarbanes-Oxley Act (2002)	Made securities fraud a criminal offense; stiffened penalties for corporate fraud; created an accounting oversight board; and instituted numerous other provisions designed to increase corporate transparency and compliance.
Do Not Call Implementation Act (2003)	Directs FCC and FTC to coordinate so their rules are consistent regarding telemarketing call practices, including the Do Not Call Registry.
Dodd-Frank Wall Street Reform and Consumer Protection Act (2010)	Increases accountability and transparency in the financial industry, protects consumers from deceptive financial practices, and establishes the Bureau of Consumer Financial Protection.

on the boards of competing corporations. The act also exempts farm cooperatives and labor organizations from antitrust laws.

In spite of these laws regulating business practices, there are still many questions about the regulation of business. For instance, it is difficult to determine what constitutes an acceptable degree of competition and whether a monopoly is harmful to a particular market. Many mergers were permitted that resulted in less competition in the banking, publishing, and automobile industries. In some industries, such as utilities, it is not cost effective to have too many competitors. For this reason, the government permits utility monopolies, although recently, the telephone, electricity, and communications industries have been deregulated. Furthermore, the antitrust laws are often rather vague and require interpretation, which may vary from judge to judge and court to court. Thus, what one judge defines as a monopoly or trust today may be permitted by another judge a few years from now. Businesspeople need to understand what the law says on these issues and try to conduct their affairs within the bounds of these laws.

互联网：法律和监管问题
The Internet: Legal and Regulatory Issues

Our use and dependence on the Internet is increasingly creating a potential legal problem for businesses. With this growing use come questions of maintaining an acceptable level of privacy for consumers and proper competitive use of the medium. Some might consider that tracking individuals who visit or "hit" their website by attaching a "cookie" (identifying you as a website visitor for potential recontact and tracking your movement throughout the site) is an improper use of the Internet for business purposes. Others may find such practices acceptable and similar to the practices of non-Internet retailers who copy information from checks or ask customers for their name, address, or phone number before they will process a transaction. There are few specific laws that regulate business on the Internet, but the standards for acceptable behavior that are reflected in the basic laws and regulations designed for traditional businesses can be applied to business on the Internet as well. One law aimed specifically at advertising on the internet is the CAN-SPAM Act of 2004. The law restricts

Whether you like it or not, Google, like Yahoo! And AOL, tracks people's web browsing patterns. By tracking the sites you visit, the companies' advertisers can aim ads targeted closer to your interests.

Consider Ethics and Social Responsibility

Marvel Comics Wins Work Made-for-Hire Copyright Case

Copyrights protect works created by the author, including artwork, writing, music, movies, and any other artistic work that is fixed or stable. However, there are exceptions in cases where the work is produced by an author hired by another party for the specific purpose of creating the work. The Copyright Act of 1909 states that any work made-for-hire belongs to the employer rather than the author.

Marvel Comics won a copyright dispute of this nature. Jack Kirby, who died in 1994, was the mind behind many of Marvel Comics' most famous characters, including Iron Man, the Incredible Hulk, and X-Men. In 2009, his children notified Marvel Comics that they intended to take back the copyrights to characters created by their father. The U.S. District Court for the Southern District of New York ruled that the characters rightfully belonged to Marvel Comics. Because Mr. Kirby was under contract, the characters fall under the definition of work made-for-hire in copyright law. His children appealed to the Second U.S. Circuit Court of Appeals. The judge again ruled that the characters belong to Marvel Comics.

The characters under consideration are profitable figures for Marvel Comics and its parent company Walt Disney. In 2013, the *Iron Man 3* movie brought in more than $400 million. It is, therefore, a high priority for Marvel to defend its intellectual property.[81]

Discussion Questions

1. According to the definition of copyright, why would comic book characters receive copyright status?
2. Why is it important for companies or individuals to defend their intellectual property?
3. Do you agree with the court's decision that Jack Kirby's characters were works made-for-hire and are thereby owned by Marvel Comics? Why or why not?

---

unsolicited e-mail advertisements by requiring the consent of the recipient. Furthermore, the CAN-SPAM Act follows the "opt-out" model wherein recipients can elect to not receive further e-mails from a sender simply by clicking on a link.[82]

The central focus for future legislation of business conducted on the Internet is the protection of personal privacy. The present basis of personal privacy protection is the U.S. Constitution, various Supreme Court rulings, and laws such as the 1971 Fair Credit Reporting Act, the 1978 Right to Financial Privacy Act, and the 1974 Privacy Act, which deals with the release of government records. With few regulations on the use of information by businesses, companies legally buy and sell information on customers to gain competitive advantage. Sometimes existing laws are not enough to protect people, and the ease with which information on customers can be obtained becomes a problem. For example, identity theft has increased due to the proliferation of the use of the Internet. A disturbing trend is how many children have had their identities stolen. One study of 40,000 children revealed that more than 10 percent have had their Social Security numbers stolen. The rates of child identity theft have risen since the advent of the Internet.[83] It has been suggested that the treatment of personal data as property will ensure privacy rights by recognizing that customers have a right to control the use of their personal data.

Internet use is different from traditional interaction with businesses in that it is readily accessible, and most online businesses are able to develop databases of information on customers. Congress has restricted the development of databases on children using the Internet. The Children's Online Privacy Protection Act of 2000 prohibits website and Internet providers from seeking personal information from children under age 13 without parental consent. Companies are still running afoul of COPPA. The Federal Trade Commission charged the social networking app Path with violating COPPA by collecting personal information from about 3,000 minors without their parents' consent. The company agreed to pay $800,000 to settle the charges.[84]

The Internet has also created a copyright dilemma for some organizations that have found that the web addresses of other online firms either match or are very similar to their company trademark. "Cybersquatters" attempt to sell back the registration of these matching sites to the trademark owner.

Companies such as Taco Bell, MTC, and KFC have paid thousands of dollars to gain control of domain names that match or parallel company trademarks. The Federal Trademark Dilution Act of 1995 helps companies address this conflict. The act provides trademark owners the right to protect trademarks, prevents the use of trademark-protected entities, and requires the relinquishment of names that match or closely parallel company trademarks. The reduction of geographic barriers, speed of response, and memory capability of the Internet will continue to create new challenges for the legal and regulatory environment in the future.

负责任商业行为的法律压力 Legal Pressure for Responsible Business Conduct

To ensure greater compliance with society's desires, both federal and state governments are moving toward increased organizational accountability for misconduct. Before 1991, laws mainly punished those employees directly responsible for an offense. Under new guidelines established by the Federal Sentencing Guidelines for Organizations (FSGO), however, both the responsible employees and the firms that employ them are held accountable for violations of federal law. Thus, the government now places responsibility for controlling and preventing misconduct squarely on the shoulders of top management. The main objectives of the federal guidelines are to train employees, self-monitor and supervise employee conduct, deter unethical acts, and punish those organizational members who engage in illegal acts.

A 2004 amendment to the FSGO requires that a business's governing authority be well informed about its ethics program with respect to content, implementation, and effectiveness. This places the responsibility on the shoulders of the firm's leadership, usually the board of directors. The board must ensure that there is a high-ranking manager accountable for the day-to-day operational oversight of the ethics program. The board must provide for adequate authority, resources, and access to the board or an appropriate subcommittee of the board. The board must ensure that there are confidential mechanisms available so that the organization's employees and agents may report or seek guidance about potential or actual misconduct without fear of retaliation. Finally, the board is required to oversee the discovery of risks and to design, implement, and modify approaches to deal with those risks.

If an organization's culture and policies reward or provide opportunities to engage in misconduct through lack of managerial concern or failure to comply with the seven minimum requirements of the FSGO (provided in Table B.4), then the organization may incur not only penalties but also the loss of customer trust, public confidence, and other intangible assets. For this reason, organizations cannot succeed solely through a legalistic approach to compliance with the sentencing guidelines; top management must cultivate high ethical standards that will serve as barriers to illegal conduct. The organization must want

TABLE B.4 Seven Steps to Compliance

1. Develop standards and procedures to reduce the propensity for criminal conduct.
2. Designate a high-level compliance manager or ethics officer to oversee the compliance program.
3. Avoid delegating authority to people known to have a propensity to engage in misconduct.
4. Communicate standards and procedures to employees, other agents, and independent contractors through training programs and publications.
5. Establish systems to monitor and audit misconduct and to allow employees and agents to report criminal activity.
6. Enforce standards and punishments consistently across all employees in the organization.
7. Respond immediately to misconduct and take reasonable steps to prevent further criminal conduct.

Source: United States Sentencing Commission, Federal Sentencing Guidelines for Organizations, *1991.*

to be a good citizen and recognize the importance of compliance to successful workplace activities and relationships.

The federal guidelines also require businesses to develop programs that can detect—and that will deter employees from engaging in—misconduct. To be considered effective, such compliance programs must include disclosure of any wrongdoing, cooperation with the government, and acceptance of responsibility for the misconduct. Codes of ethics, employee ethics training, hotlines (direct 800 phone numbers), compliance directors, newsletters, brochures, and other communication methods are typical components of a compliance program. The ethics component, discussed in Chapter 2, acts as a buffer, keeping firms away from the thin line that separates unethical and illegal conduct.

Despite the existing legislation, a number of ethics scandals in the early 2000s led Congress to pass—almost unanimously—the **Sarbanes-Oxley Act,** which criminalized securities fraud and strengthened penalties for corporate fraud. It also created an accounting oversight board that requires corporations to establish codes of ethics for financial reporting and to develop greater transparency in financial reports to investors and other interested parties. Additionally, the law requires top corporate executives to sign off on their firms' financial reports, and they risk fines and jail sentences if they misrepresent their companies' financial position. Table B.5 summarizes the major provisions of the Sarbanes-Oxley Act.

The Sarbanes-Oxley Act has created a number of concerns and is considered burdensome and expensive to corporations. Large corporations report spending more than $4 million each year to comply with the Act according to Financial Executives International. The Act has caused more than 500 public companies a year to report problems in their accounting systems.

TABLE B.5 Major Provisions of the Sarbanes-Oxley Act

1. Requires the establishment of a Public Company Accounting Oversight Board in charge of regulations administered by the Securities and Exchange Commission.
2. Requires CEOs and CFOs to certify that their companies' financial statements are true and without misleading statements.
3. Requires that corporate boards of directors' audit committees consist of independent members who have no material interests in the company.
4. Prohibits corporations from making or offering loans to officers and board members.
5. Requires codes of ethics for senior financial officers; code must be registered with the SEC.
6. Prohibits accounting firms from providing both auditing and consulting services to the same client without the approval of the client firm's audit committee.
7. Requires company attorneys to report wrongdoing to top managers and, if necessary, to the board of directors; if managers and directors fail to respond to reports of wrongdoing, the attorney should stop representing the company.
8. Mandates "whistleblower protection" for persons who disclose wrongdoing to authorities.
9. Requires financial securities analysts to certify that their recommendations are based on objective reports.
10. Requires mutual fund managers to disclose how they vote shareholder proxies, giving investors information about how their shares influence decisions.
11. Establishes a 10-year penalty for mail/wire fraud.
12. Prohibits the two senior auditors from working on a corporation's account for more than five years; other auditors are prohibited from working on an account for more than seven years. In other words, accounting firms must rotate individual auditors from one account to another from time to time.

Source: Pub. L. 107-204, 116 Stat. 745 (2002).

Additionally, Sarbanes-Oxley failed to prevent and detect the widespread misconduct of financial institutions that led to the financial crisis.

On the other hand, there are many benefits, including greater accountability of top managers and boards of directors, that improve investor confidence and protect employees, especially their retirement plans. It is believed that the law has more benefits than drawbacks—with the greatest benefit being that boards of directors and top managers are better informed. Some companies such as Cisco and Pitney Bowes report improved efficiency and cost savings from better financial information.

In spite of the benefits Sarbanes-Oxley offers, it did not prevent widespread corporate corruption from leading to the most recent recession. The resulting financial crisis prompted the Obama administration to create new regulation to reform Wall Street and the financial industry. In 2010, the Dodd-Frank Wall Street Reform and Consumer Protection Act was passed. In addition to new regulations for financial institutions, the legislation created a Consumer Financial Protection Bureau (CFPB) to protect consumers from complex or deceptive financial products. Table B.6 highlights some of the major provisions of the Dodd-Frank Act.

The Dodd-Frank Act contains 16 titles meant to increase consumer protection, enhance transparency and accountability in the financial sector, and create new financial agencies. In some ways, Dodd-Frank is attempting to improve upon provisions laid out in the Sarbanes-Oxley Act. For instance, Dodd-Frank takes whistleblower protection a step further by offering additional incentives to whistleblowers for reporting

TABLE B.6 Major Provisions of the Dodd-Frank Wall Street Reform and Consumer Protection Act

1.	Enhances stability of the finance industry through the creation of two new financial agencies, the Financial Oversight Stability Council and the Office of Financial Research.
2.	Institutes an orderly liquidation procedure for the Federal Deposit Insurance Corporation to liquidate failing companies.
3.	Eliminates the Office of Thrift Supervision and transfers its powers to the Comptroller of the Currency.
4.	Creates stronger regulation and greater oversight of hedge funds.
5.	Establishes the Federal Insurance Agency to gather information and oversee the insurance industry for risks.
6.	Requires regulators to have regulations in place for banks. Also prohibits and/or limits proprietary trading, hedge fund sponsorship and private equity funds, and relationships with hedge funds and private equity funds.
7.	Regulates derivatives and complex financial instruments by limiting where they can be traded and ensuring that traders have the financial resources to meet their responsibilities.
8.	Provides a framework for creating risk-management standards for financial market utilities and the payment, clearing, and settlement activities performed by institutions.
9.	Improves investor protection through acts such as creating a whistleblower bounty program and increasing consumer access to their credit scores.
10.	Institutes the Bureau of Consumer Financial Protection to educate consumers and protect them from deceptive financial products.
11.	Attempts to reform the Federal Reserve in ways that include limiting the Federal Reserve's lending authority, reevaluating methods for Federal Reserve regulations and the appointment of Federal Reserve Bank directors, and instituting additional disclosure requirements.
12.	Reforms mortgage activities with new provisions that include increasing the lender's responsibility to ensure the borrower can pay back the loan, prohibiting unfair lending practices, requiring additional disclosure in the mortgage loan process, and imposing penalties against those found guilty of noncompliance with the new standards.

Source: Brief Summary of the Dodd-Frank Wall Street Reform and Consumer Protection Act.

misconduct. If whistleblowers report misconduct that results in penalties of more than $1 million, the whistleblower will be entitled to a percentage of the settlement.[85] Additionally, complex financial instruments must now be made more transparent so that consumers will have a better understanding of what these instruments involve.

The act also created three new agencies: the Consumer Financial Protection Bureau (CFPB), the Office of Financial Research, and the Financial Stability Oversight Council. While the CFPB was created to protect consumers, the other two agencies work to maintain stability in the financial industry so such a crisis will not recur in the future.[86] Although it is too early to tell whether these regulations will serve to create widescale positive financial reform, the Dodd-Frank Act is certainly leading to major changes on Wall Street and in the financial sector.

3

Business in a Borderless World
无边界世界中的商业

Learning Objectives

After reading this chapter, you will be able to:

LO 3-1 Explore some of the factors within the international trade environment that influence business.

LO 3-2 Investigate some of the economic, legal, political, social, cultural, and technological barriers to international business.

LO 3-3 Specify some of the agreements, alliances, and organizations that may encourage trade across international boundaries.

LO 3-4 Summarize the different levels of organizational involvement in international trade.

LO 3-5 Contrast two basic strategies used in international business.

LO 3-6 Assess the opportunities and problems facing a small business that is considering expanding into international markets.

Chapter Outline

进入商业世界

Enter the World of Business

中国智能手机公司面临扩张挑战

Chinese Smartphone Company Faces Challenges in Expansion

Xiaomi, China's hottest smartphone company, has established itself as an icon of innovation. Founded in 2010 by entrepreneur Lei Jun—who has been called "the Steve Jobs of China"—the company is already valued at more than $10 billion and is expanding into global markets. So far, the company has seen increasing growth opportunities. However, this potential does not exist in all markets, especially in those where Apple and Samsung dominate the market.

The company is looking into ways of entering the United States, but many barriers to entry exist. A strength that Xiaomi has over competitors in China is its ability to create a high-quality, low-priced phone that appeals to the average Chinese consumer. This may not matter as much to Americans, who are willing to pay a premium for Apple and Samsung brands. Xiaomi's brand image, which is perceived as cool, hip, and cheap, could be tarnished in China if it is successful and becomes a global brand. More practically, getting the phones into retail locations may prove troublesome to the small cell phone maker. In the United States, cell phone companies must negotiate contracts with service providers, which is not the case in China. This process is highly competitive and hard for new entrants to break into. Another difficulty is the name of the company itself, as many Americans are not able to say Xiaomi (sheow me).

引言
Introduction

Consumers around the world can drink Coca-Cola and Pepsi; eat at McDonald's and Pizza Hut; see movies from Mexico, England, France, Australia, and China; and watch CNN and MTV on Samsung televisions. It may surprise you that the Japanese firm Komatsu sells earth-moving equipment to China that is manufactured in Peoria, Illinois.[2] The products you consume today are just as likely to have been made in China, India, or Germany as in the United States.[4] Likewise, consumers in other countries buy Western electrical equipment, clothing, rock music, cosmetics, and toiletries, as well as computers, robots, and household goods.

DID YOU KNOW? **Subway has surpassed McDonald's as the largest global restaurant chain with more than 41,000 restaurants.**[3]

Many U.S. firms are finding that international markets provide tremendous opportunities for growth. Accessing these markets can promote innovation while intensifying global competition spurs companies to market better and less expensive products. Today, the more than 7 billion people that inhabit the earth comprise one tremendous marketplace.

国际商务
international business the buying, selling, and trading of goods and services across national boundaries

In this chapter, we explore business in this exciting global marketplace. First, we look at the nature of international business, including barriers and promoters of trade across international boundaries. Next, we consider the levels of organizational involvement in international business. Finally, we briefly discuss strategies for trading across national borders.

国际商务的作用
The Role of International Business

International business refers to the buying, selling, and trading of goods and services across national boundaries. Falling political barriers and new technology are making it possible for more and more companies to sell their products overseas as well as at home. And, as differences among nations continue to narrow, the trend toward the globalization of business is becoming increasingly important. Starbucks serves millions of global customers at more than 19,000 locations in 62 countries.[5] The Internet and the ease by which mobile applications can be developed provides many companies with easier entry to access global markets than opening bricks-and-mortar stores.[6] Amazon.com, an online retailer, has distribution centers from Nevada to Germany that fill millions of orders a day and ship them to customers in every corner of the world. The Apple Store surpassed $10 billion in app sales alone in 2013. A total of $1 billion came into the company over a one-month period shortly after Apple released a new operating system. More than 70 percent of revenues from Apple stores came from outside of the United States.[7] Indeed, most of the world's population and two-thirds of its total purchasing power are outside the United States.

American companies such as McDonald's have become widely popular in China. This restaurant in Beijing features elements from the Chinese culture as well as from American culture.

When McDonald's sells a Big Mac in Moscow, Sony sells a stereo in Detroit, or a small Swiss medical supply company sells a shipment of orthopedic devices to a hospital in Monterrey, Mexico, the sale affects the economies of the countries involved. The U.S. market, with 316 million consumers, makes up only a small part of the more than 7 billion people elsewhere in the world to whom global companies must consider marketing.[8] Global marketing requires balancing your global brand with the needs of local consumers.[9] To begin our study of international business, we must first consider some economic issues: why nations trade, exporting and importing, and the balance of trade.

Many companies choose to outsource manufacturing to factories in Asia due to lower costs of labor.

为什么要进行国际贸易
Why Nations Trade

Nations and businesses engage in international trade to obtain raw materials and goods that are otherwise unavailable to them or are available elsewhere at a lower price than that at which they themselves can produce. A nation, or individuals and organizations from a nation, sell surplus materials and goods to acquire funds to buy the goods, services, and ideas its people need. Poland, for example, began trading with Western nations in order to acquire new technology and techniques. Poland has taken these lessons and revitalized its formerly communist economy.[10] Which goods and services a nation sells depends on what resources it has available.

Some nations have a monopoly on the production of a particular resource or product. Such a monopoly, or **absolute advantage,** exists when a country is the only source of an item, the only producer of an item, or the most efficient producer of an item. Utility distribution companies are often natural monopolies out of necessity, whether they are regulated by governments or privately owned.[11] Mexico, until recently, held an absolute advantage in oil production. However, because the country was not able to produce as much crude oil as its capacity allowed, President Pena Nieto nullified the monopoly so other companies can enter the country and make use of Mexico's resources.[12]

绝对优势
absolute advantage
a monopoly that exists when a country is the only source of an item, the only producer of an item, or the most efficient producer of an item

Most international trade is based on **comparative advantage,** which occurs when a country specializes in products that it can supply more efficiently or at a lower cost than it can produce other items. Kenya has a comparative advantage in its use of mobile money, which involves payment services through mobile devices. Its use of mobile money has increased consumer convenience in completing everyday tasks. This advantage has served to modernize the country.[13] The United States, having adopted new technological methods in hydraulic fracturing, has created a comparative advantage in the mining and exporting of natural gas.[14] Other countries, particularly India and Ireland, are also gaining a comparative advantage over the United States in the provision of some services, such as call-center operations, engineering, and software programming. As a result, U.S. companies are increasingly **outsourcing,** or transferring manufacturing and other tasks to countries where labor and supplies are less expensive. Outsourcing has become a controversial practice in the United States because many jobs have moved overseas where those tasks can be accomplished for lower costs. For example, the Philippines has surpassed India as the popular choice for call-center jobs. Call-center jobs are appealing to many Filipinos because the pay is almost as much as the average family income within the country. English is also one of the country's official languages, which makes it easier to communicate with English-speaking customers.[15]

比较优势
comparative advantage
the basis of most international trade, when a country specializes in products that it can supply more efficiently or at a lower cost than it can produce other items

外包
outsourcing
the transferring of manufacturing or other tasks—such as data processing—to countries where labor and supplies are less expensive

国家之间的贸易
Trade between Countries

出口
exporting
the sale of goods and services to foreign markets

To obtain needed goods and services and the funds to pay for them, nations trade by exporting and importing. **Exporting** is the sale of goods and services to foreign markets. The United States exported more than $2.3 trillion in goods and services in 2013.[16] In China, Tesla Motors Inc. is working to implement charging stations for electric vehicles (EVs) for its exports as well as for use by Chinese-made EVs. U.S. companies that view China as both a growth market for exports and a market for lower-cost labor for imports can strategically integrate these into their operations. Successful integration can lead to significantly higher profits than companies that only focus on one of the opportunities. Apple, for example, designed a less expensive version of the iPhone for the Chinese smartphone market, while also utilizing Chinese resources for manufacturing.[17] U.S. businesses export many goods and services, particularly agricultural, entertainment (movies, television shows, etc.), and technological products. **Importing** is the purchase of goods and services from foreign sources. Many of the goods you buy in the United States are likely to be imports or to have some imported components. Sometimes, you may not even realize they are imports. The United States imported more than $2.7 trillion in goods and services in 2013.[18]

进口
importing
the purchase of goods and services from foreign sources

connect

Need help understanding Balance of Trade? Visit your Connect ebook video tab for a brief animated explanation.

贸易余额
Balance of Trade

贸易余额
balance of trade
the difference in value between a nation's exports and its imports

贸易逆差
trade deficit
a nation's negative balance of trade, which exists when that country imports more products than it exports

国际收支平衡表
balance of payments
the difference between the flow of money into and out of a country

You have probably read or heard about the fact that the United States has a trade deficit, but what is a trade deficit? A nation's **balance of trade** is the difference in value between its exports and imports. Because the United States (and some other nations as well) imports more products than it exports, it has a negative balance of trade, or **trade deficit.** Table 3.1 shows the trade deficit for the United States. In 2013, the United States had a trade deficit of more than $471 billion.[19] The trade deficit fluctuates according to such factors as the health of the United States and other economies, productivity, perceived quality, and exchange rates. As Figure 3.1 indicates, U.S. exports to China have been rapidly increasing but not fast enough to offset the imports from China. Trade deficits are harmful because they can mean the failure of businesses, the loss of jobs, and a lowered standard of living.

Of course, when a nation exports more goods than it imports, it has a favorable balance of trade, or trade surplus. Until about 1970, the United States had a trade surplus due to an abundance of natural resources and the relative efficiency of its manufacturing systems. Table 3.2 shows the top 10 countries and areas with which the United States has a trade deficit and a trade surplus.

The difference between the flow of money into and out of a country is called its **balance of payments.** A country's balance of trade, foreign investments, foreign aid,

TABLE 3.1 U.S. Trade Deficit, 1980–2006 (in billions of dollars)

	1990	2000	2007	2008	2009	2010	2011	2012	2013
Exports	535.2	1,072.8	1,652.9	1,840.3	1,578.2	1,844.5	2,112.8	2,210.6	2,272.3
Imports	616.1	1,450.1	2,351.9	2,542.6	1,961.8	2,343.8	2,669.7	2,745.2	2,743.9
Trade surplus/deficit	−80.9	−377.3	−699.1	−702.3	−383.7	−499.4	−556.8	−534.7	−471.5

Sources: U.S. Bureau of the Census, Foreign Trade Division, U.S. Trade in Goods and Services—Balance of Payments (BOP) Basis, *February 6, 2014.*

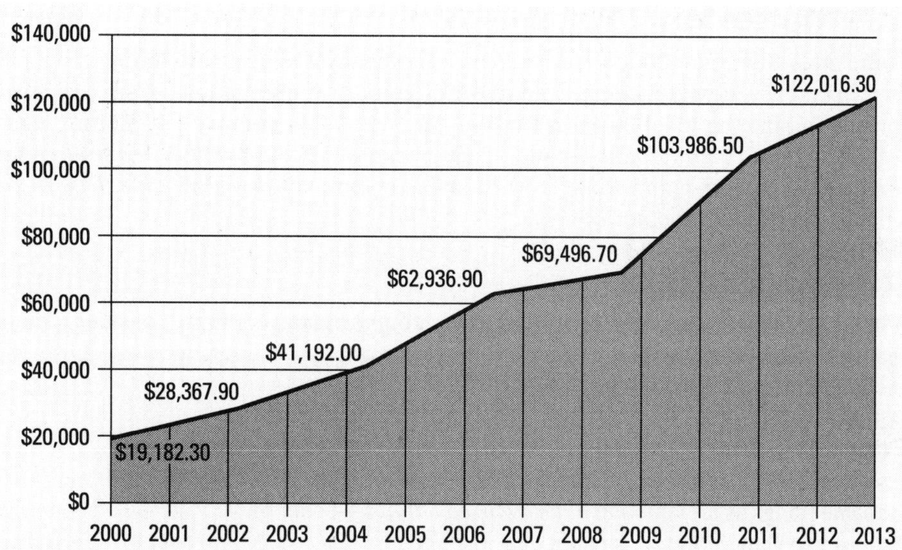

FIGURE 3.1
U.S. Exports to China (millions of U.S. dollars)

Sources: "Trade in Goods (Imports, Exports and Trade Balance) with China," U.S. Census Bureau: Foreign Trade Statistics.

TABLE 3.2
Top Ten with Which the United States Has Trade Deficits/ Surpluses

Trade Deficit	Trade Surplus
1. China	Chinese Hong Kong
2. Japan	United Arab Emirates
3. Germany	Netherlands
4. Mexico	Switzerland
5. Saudi Arabia	Belgium
6. Canada	Brazil
7. India	Australia
8. Ireland	Panama
9. South Korea	Singapore
10. Italy	Argentina

Sources: "Top Ten with which the U.S. has a Trade Deficit," April 2013; "Top Ten with which the U.S. has a Trade Surplus," April 2013.

loans, military expenditures, and money spent by tourists comprise its balance of payments. As you might expect, a country with a trade surplus generally has a favorable balance of payments because it is receiving more money from trade with foreign countries than it is paying out. When a country has a trade deficit, more money flows out of the country than into it. If more money flows out of the country than into it from tourism and other sources, the country may experience declining production and higher unemployment, because there is less money available for spending.

国际贸易壁垒
International Trade Barriers

Completely free trade seldom exists. When a company decides to do business outside its own country, it will encounter a number of barriers to international trade. Any firm considering international business must research the other country's economic, legal, political, social, cultural, and technological background. Such research will help the company choose an appropriate level of involvement and operating strategies, as we will see later in this chapter.

LO 3-2

经济壁垒
Economic Barriers

When looking at doing business in another country, managers must consider a number of basic economic factors, such as economic development, infrastructure, and exchange rates.

经济发展

Economic Development. When considering doing business abroad, U.S. businesspeople need to recognize that they cannot take for granted that other countries offer the same things as are found in *industrialized nations*—economically advanced countries such as the United States, Japan, Great Britain, and Canada. Many countries in Africa, Asia, and South America, for example, are in general poorer and less economically advanced than those in North America and Europe; they are often called *less-developed countries* (LDCs). LDCs are characterized by low per-capita income (income generated by the nation's production of goods and services divided by the population), which means that consumers are less likely to purchase nonessential products. Nonetheless, LDCs represent a potentially huge and profitable market for many businesses because they may be buying technology to improve their infrastructures, and much of the population may desire consumer products. For example, automobile manufacturers are looking toward LDCs as a way to expand their customer base. The rising middle class has caused many consumers in India and China to desire their own vehicles. Companies such as General Motors are partnering with domestic manufacturers to create electric vehicles for the Chinese market.[20]

基础建设
infrastructure
the physical facilities that support a country's economic activities, such as railroads, highways, ports, airfields, utilities and power plants, schools, hospitals, communication systems, and commercial distribution systems

A country's level of development is determined in part by its **infrastructure,** the physical facilities that support its economic activities, such as railroads, highways, ports, airfields, utilities and power plants, schools, hospitals, communication systems, and commercial distribution systems. When doing business in LDCs, for example, a business may need to compensate for rudimentary distribution and communication systems, or even a lack of technology.

汇率
exchange rate
the ratio at which one nation's currency can be exchanged for another nation's currency

汇率

Exchange Rates. The ratio at which one nation's currency can be exchanged for another nation's currency is the **exchange rate.** Exchange rates vary daily and can be found in newspapers and through many sites on the Internet. Familiarity with exchange rates is important because they affect the cost of imports and exports. When the value of the U.S. dollar declines relative to other currencies, such as the euro, the price of imports becomes relatively expensive for U.S. consumers. On the other hand, U.S. exports become relatively cheap for international markets—in this example, the European Union (EU).

Occasionally, a government may intentionally alter the value of its currency through fiscal policy. Devaluation decreases the value of currency in relation to other currencies. If the U.S. government were to devalue the dollar, it would lower the cost of American goods abroad and make trips to the United States less expensive for foreign tourists. Thus, devaluation encourages the sale of domestic goods and tourism. Mexico has repeatedly devalued the peso for this reason. China has

Going Green

China's Sustainability Initiatives

Over the past 10 years, China's sustainable energy initiatives have become significant. As a country that is home to much of the world's industrial production, China began experiencing an onslaught of detrimental consequences such as brownouts (when pollution becomes so saturated in the air that it inhibits vision), blackouts due to lack of adequate energy to supply demand, acid rain, and nonpotable water. Urbanization also became a contributing factor when people began migrating from rural areas to cities at a rate of 20 million annually. As people move into cities and grow into the middle class, they tend to purchase larger houses and more automobiles that demand the use of more energy.

To correct the negative environmental impact, China has begun many sustainable initiatives to diversify its energy sources from coal (80 percent of Chinese energy comes from coal) to cleaner alternatives. The government has eliminated inefficient industrial programs, raised the minimum efficiency standards for construction methods, and instituted automobile fuel economy standards. The Chinese government also began designing policies and programs by which to standardize initiatives and monitor their progress through green labeling practices. Investments in technology research related to biofuels, solar, wind farms, carbon capture, and more are a part of this corrective action. As a result, energy consumption has fallen more than 20 percent, and China has become a world leader in wind power capacity.[21]

Discussion Questions

1. What are some of the problems China has faced due to pollution?
2. Why does a rising middle class potentially threaten the environment?
3. Describe some of the ways that the Chinese government is tackling the pollution issue.

been accused of devaluing the yuan as exports for the country have reached historical lows.[22] Revaluation, which increases the value of a currency in relation to other currencies, occurs rarely.

道德、法律和政治壁垒

Ethical, Legal, and Political Barriers

A company that decides to enter the international marketplace must contend with potentially complex relationships among the different laws of its own nation, international laws, and the laws of the nation with which it will be trading; various trade restrictions imposed on international trade; changing political climates; and different ethical values. Legal and ethical requirements for successful business are increasing globally. For instance, India has strict limitations on foreign retailers that want to operate within the country. Until recently, foreign retailers were required to partner with a domestic firm if they wanted to do business within India. Walmart partnered with Bharti Enterprises in order to gain entry into the country. However, this five-year partnership came to an end after Walmart decided that navigating through Indian restrictions was too cumbersome and resulted in little progress. Internet legislation in other countries is causing some companies to pause out of concern. Brazil has proposed a bill dictating that Internet companies that offer services in the country, such as Google and Yahoo!, buy local data storage space to keep data within the country. If the bill passes, the result is significant extra costs that could serve as a deterrent to foreign investment.[23]

法律与监管

Laws and Regulations. The United States has a number of laws and regulations that govern the activities of U.S. firms engaged in international trade. For example, the Webb-Pomerene Export Trade Act of 1918 exempts American firms from antitrust laws if those firms are acting together to enter international trade. This law

Counterfeit products such as these fake luxury handbags are major challenges for international firms.

allows selected U.S. firms to form monopolies to compete with foreign monopolistic organizations, although they are not allowed to limit free trade and competition within the United States or to use unfair methods of competition in international trade. The United States also has a variety of friendship, commerce, and navigation treaties with other nations. These treaties allow business to be transacted between citizens of the specified countries. Ireland is an up-and-coming example of a country that attracts American foreign investment. Corporate tax rates that are among the lowest in Europe, low wages, and sufficient infrastructure are just a few of the reasons investors are attracted to Ireland. Over the course of 2008 to 2012, American investment in the country totaled $129.5 billion—more than the prior 58 years combined.[24]

Once outside U.S. borders, businesspeople are likely to find that the laws of other nations differ from those of the United States. Many of the legal rights that Americans take for granted do not exist in other countries, and a firm doing business abroad must understand and obey the laws of the host country. Some countries have strict laws limiting the amount of local currency that can be taken out of the country and the amount of currency that can be brought in; others limit how foreign companies can operate within the country.

In Mexico, for example, foreigners cannot directly own property in what is known as the "Restricted Zone." The Restricted Zone includes land within 100 kilometers of Mexico's international borders along with land within 50 kilometers of Mexico's oceans and beaches. Foreigners who wish to use property in these areas must obtain a title through a bank title transfer or through a corporation.[25]

Some countries have copyright and patent laws that are less strict than those of the United States, and some countries fail to honor U.S. laws. It is estimated that nearly half of all software installed on personal computers worldwide is illegally pirated or copied.[26] In countries where these activities occur, laws against them may not be sufficiently enforced if counterfeiting is deemed illegal. Thus, businesses engaging in foreign trade may have to take extra steps to protect their products because local laws may be insufficient to do so.

关税与贸易限制

Tariffs and Trade Restrictions. Tariffs and other trade restrictions are part of a country's legal structure but may be established or removed for political reasons. An **import tariff** is a tax levied by a nation on goods imported into the country. A *fixed tariff* is a specific amount of money levied on each unit of a product brought into the country, while an *ad valorem tariff* is based on the value of the item. Most countries allow citizens traveling abroad to bring home a certain amount of merchandise without paying an import tariff. A U.S. citizen may bring $200 worth of merchandise into

进口关税
import tariff
a tax levied by a nation on goods imported into the country

the United States duty free. After that, U.S. citizens must pay an ad valorem tariff based on the cost of the item and the country of origin. Thus, identical items purchased in different countries might have different tariffs.

Countries sometimes levy tariffs for political reasons, as when they impose sanctions against other countries to protest their actions. However, import tariffs are more commonly imposed to protect domestic products by raising the price of imported ones. Such protective tariffs have become controversial, as Americans become increasingly concerned over the U.S. trade deficit. Protective tariffs allow more expensive domestic goods to compete with foreign ones. For example, the United States has lost a significant number of steelworks over the past few decades to foreign competition in places such as China. Other markets can produce steel more cheaply than the United States. Many people and special interest groups in the United States, such as unions, would like to see tariffs placed on Chinese steel, which is significantly less expensive, in order to protect remaining U.S. steel production. The United States has also imposed tariffs on imported sugar for almost two centuries. The EU levies tariffs on many products, including some seafood imports.

Due to the U.S. embargo against Cuba, many Cubans drive older automobiles.

Critics of protective tariffs argue that their use inhibits free trade and competition. Supporters of protective tariffs say they insulate domestic industries, particularly new ones, against well-established foreign competitors. Once an industry matures, however, its advocates may be reluctant to let go of the tariff that protected it. Tariffs also help when, because of low labor costs and other advantages, foreign competitors can afford to sell their products at prices lower than those charged by domestic companies. Some Americans argue that tariffs should be used to keep domestic wages high and unemployment low.

外汇管制
exchange controls
regulations that restrict the amount of currency that can be bought or sold

Exchange controls restrict the amount of currency that can be bought or sold. Some countries control their foreign trade by forcing businesspeople to buy and sell foreign products through a central bank. If John Deere, for example, receives payments for its tractors in a foreign currency, it may be required to sell the currency to that nation's central bank. When foreign currency is in short supply, as it is in many LDCs, the government uses foreign currency to purchase necessities and capital goods and produces other products locally, thus limiting its need for foreign imports.

进口配额
quota
a restriction on the number of units of a particular product that can be imported into a country

A **quota** limits the number of units of a particular product that can be imported into a country. A quota may be established by voluntary agreement or by government decree. The United States imposes quotas on certain goods, such as garments produced in Vietnam and China. Quotas are designed to protect the industries and jobs of the country imposing the quota.

禁运
embargo
a prohibition on trade in a particular product

An **embargo** prohibits trade in a particular product. Embargoes are generally directed at specific goods or countries and may be established for political, economic, health, or religious reasons. While the United States maintains a trade embargo with Cuba, European hotel chains are engaged in a building boom on the Caribbean island, where tourism is the number-one industry. U.S. hotel chains are eager to build in Cuba but have no opportunity until the embargo is lifted. Until recently, U.S. tourists were forbidden by the U.S. government to vacation in Cuba because of the embargo. However, the government has begun to allow more Americans to visit Cuba with certain restrictions.[27] It may be surprising to know that U.S. farmers export hundreds of millions of dollars worth of commodities to Cuba each year, based on a 2000 law that provided permission for some trade to the embargoed country.[28] Health embargoes prevent the importing of various pharmaceuticals, animals, plants, and agricultural products. Muslim nations forbid the importation of alcoholic beverages on religious grounds.

倾销
dumping
the act of a country or business selling products at less than what it costs to produce them

One common reason for setting quotas or tariffs is to prohibit **dumping,** which occurs when a country or business sells products at less than what it costs to produce them. For example, in 2013 the U.S. Immigration and Customs Enforcement, along with Homeland Security Investigations, charged Honey Solutions and Groeb Farms Inc. with dumping violations concerning honey imports from China.[29] A company may dump its products for several reasons. Dumping permits quick entry into a market. Sometimes dumping occurs when the domestic market for a firm's product is too small to support an efficient level of production. In other cases, technologically obsolete products that are no longer salable in the country of origin are dumped overseas. Dumping is relatively difficult to prove, but even the suspicion of dumping can lead to the imposition of quotas or tariffs. Honey Solutions paid $1 million in fines, while Groeb Farms Inc. agreed to pay $2 million at this point in the prosecution.[30]

政治壁垒

Political Barriers. Unlike legal issues, political considerations are seldom written down and often change rapidly. Nations that have been subject to economic sanctions for political reasons in recent years include Cuba, Iran, Syria, and North Korea. While these were dramatic events, political considerations affect international business daily as governments enact tariffs, embargoes, or other types of trade restrictions in response to political events.

A European complaint has alleged that China is dumping solar panels and urges the EU to implement import tariffs. China denies any such activity.

Businesses engaged in international trade must consider the relative instability of countries such as Iraq, Ukraine, and Venezuela. Political unrest in countries such as Pakistan, Somalia, and the Democratic Republic of the Congo may create a hostile or even dangerous environment for foreign businesses. Natural disasters, like the 2013 typhoons in the Philippines and India,[31] can cripple a country's government, making the region even more unstable. Even a developed country such as Japan had its social, economic, and political institutions stressed by the 2011 earthquake and tsunamis. Finally, a sudden change in power can result in a regime that is hostile to foreign investment. Some businesses have been forced out of a country altogether, as when Hugo Chávez conducted a socialist revolution in Venezuela to force out or take over American oil companies. Whether they like it or not, companies are often involved directly or indirectly in international politics.

Political concerns may lead a group of nations to form a **cartel,** a group of firms or nations that agrees to act as a monopoly and not compete with each other, to generate a competitive advantage in world markets. Probably the most famous cartel is OPEC, the Organization of Petroleum Exporting Countries, founded in the 1960s to increase the price of petroleum throughout the world and to maintain high prices. By working to ensure stable oil prices, OPEC hopes to enhance the economies of its member nations.

垄断联盟
cartel
a group of firms or nations that agrees to act as a monopoly and not compete with each other, in order to generate a competitive advantage in world markets

社会与文化壁垒
Social and Cultural Barriers

Most businesspeople engaged in international trade underestimate the importance of social and cultural differences; but these differences can derail an important transaction. Burger King recently formed a joint venture with Everstone Group to begin opening locations in India. The fast-food chain can take lessons from already established competitors that learned the necessity of adapting their menus to reflect the religious and social customs of the region.[32] Additionally, Tiffany & Co. learned that more attentive customer service was necessary in order to succeed in Japan, and bold marketing and advertising served as the recipe for success in China.[33] And in Europe, Starbucks took the unprecedented step of allowing its locations to be franchised in order to reach smaller markets that are unfamiliar. This way Starbucks reduced some of the cultural and social risks involved in entering such markets.[34] Unfortunately, cultural norms are rarely written down, and what is written down may well be inaccurate.

Cultural differences include differences in spoken and written language. Although it is certainly possible to translate words from one language to another, the true meaning is sometimes misinterpreted or lost. Consider some translations that went awry in foreign markets:

- Scandinavian vacuum manufacturer Electrolux used the following in an American campaign: "Nothing sucks like an Electrolux."
- The Coca-Cola name in China was first read as "Ke-kou-ke-la," meaning "bite the wax tadpole."
- In Italy, a campaign for Schweppes Tonic Water translated the name into Schweppes Toilet Water.[35]

Translators cannot just translate slogans, advertising campaigns, and website language; they must know the cultural differences that could affect a company's success.

Differences in body language and personal space also affect international trade. Body language is nonverbal, usually unconscious communication through gestures, posture, and facial expression. Personal space is the distance at which one person feels comfortable talking to another. Americans tend to stand a moderate distance away from the person with whom they are speaking. Arab businessmen tend to stand face-to-face with the object of their conversation. Additionally, gestures vary from culture to culture, and gestures considered acceptable in American society—pointing, for example—may be considered rude in others. Table 3.3 shows some of the behaviors considered rude or unacceptable in other countries. Such cultural differences may generate uncomfortable feelings or misunderstandings when businesspeople of different countries negotiate with each other.

TABLE 3.3
Cultural Behavioral Differences

Region	Gestures Viewed as Rude or Unacceptable
Japan, Middle East	Summoning with the index finger
Middle and Far East	Pointing with index finger
Thailand, Japan, France	Sitting with soles of shoes showing
Brazil, Germany	Forming a circle with fingers (the "O.K." sign in the United States)
Japan	Winking means "I love you"
Buddhist countries	Patting someone on the head

Source: Adapted from Judie Haynes, "Communicating with Gestures," EverythingESL *(n.d.).*

Family roles also influence marketing activities. Many countries do not allow children to be used in advertising, for example. Advertising that features people in nontraditional social roles may or may not be successful either. Fine Indian jeweler Tanishq was criticized for an advertisement aired in its native country. The advertisement depicted a marriage ceremony between a single mother and a man who was obviously not the father of the child. Critics claimed the ad disregarded Indian values and morals because widowed and divorced women are often shunned from their communities. Remarriage and premarital relations, under any circumstances, are not appropriate in Indian culture. Others saw the ad starting a conversation about women's rights.[36]

The people of other nations quite often have a different perception of time as well. Americans value promptness; a business meeting scheduled for a specific time seldom starts more than a few minutes late. In Mexico and Spain, however, it is not unusual for a meeting to be delayed half an hour or more. Such a late start might produce resentment in an American negotiating in Spain for the first time.

Companies engaged in foreign trade must observe the national and religious holidays and local customs of the host country. In many Islamic countries, for example, workers expect to take a break at certain times of the day to observe religious rites. Companies also must monitor their advertising to guard against offending customers. In Thailand and many other countries, public displays of affection between the sexes are unacceptable in advertising messages; in many Middle Eastern nations, it is unacceptable to show the soles of one's feet.[37] In Russia, smiling is considered appropriate only in private settings, not in business.

With the exception of the United States, most nations use the metric system. This lack of uniformity creates problems for both buyers and sellers in the international marketplace. American sellers, for instance, must package goods destined for foreign markets in liters or meters, and Japanese sellers must convert to the English system if they plan to sell a product in the United States. Tools also must be calibrated in the correct system if they are to function correctly. Hyundai and Honda service technicians need metric tools to make repairs on those cars.

The literature dealing with international business is filled with accounts of sometimes humorous but often costly mistakes that occurred because of a lack of understanding of the social and cultural differences between buyers and sellers. Such problems cannot always be avoided, but they can be minimized through research on the cultural and social differences of the host country.

科技壁垒
Technological Barriers

Cell phone services are taking off in Africa. They offer a viable alternative to landlines, which require infrastructure not always available in rural areas.

Many countries lack the technological infrastructure found in the United States, and some marketers are viewing such barriers as opportunities. For instance, marketers are targeting many countries such as India and some African countries where there are few private phone lines. Citizens of these countries are turning instead to wireless communication through cell phones. Technological advances are creating additional global marketing opportunities. Along with opportunities, changing technologies also create new challenges and competition. The U.S. market share of the personal computer market is dropping as new competitors emerge that are challenging U.S. PC makers. In fact, out of the top five global PC companies—Lenovo, Hewlett-Packard, Dell, Acer Group, and ASUS—three are from Asian countries. On the other hand, Apple Inc.'s iPad and other tablet computer makers have already begun eroding the market share of traditional personal computers, leading many to believe that personal computers have hit the maturity stage of the product life cycle.[38]

贸易协定、联盟与组织
Trade Agreements, Alliances, and Organizations

LO 3-3

Although these economic, political, legal, and sociocultural issues may seem like daunting barriers to international trade, there are also organizations and agreements—such as the General Agreement on Tariffs and Trade, the World Bank, and the International Monetary Fund—that foster international trade and can help companies get involved in and succeed in global markets. Various regional trade agreements, such as the North American Free Trade Agreement and the EU, also promote trade among member nations by eliminating tariffs and trade restrictions. In this section, we'll look briefly at these agreements and organizations.

关税及贸易总协定
General Agreement on Tariffs and Trade

During the Great Depression of the 1930s, nations established so many protective tariffs covering so many products that international trade became virtually impossible. By the end of World War II, there was considerable international momentum to liberalize trade and minimize the effects of tariffs. The **General Agreement on Tariffs and Trade (GATT),** originally signed by 23 nations in 1947, provided a forum for tariff negotiations and a place where international trade problems could be discussed and resolved. More than 100 nations abided by its rules. GATT sponsored rounds of negotiations aimed at reducing trade restrictions. The most recent round, the Uruguay Round (1988–1994), further reduced trade barriers for most products and provided new rules to prevent dumping.

The **World Trade Organization (WTO),** an international organization dealing with the rules of trade between nations, was created in 1995 by the Uruguay Round. Key to the World Trade Organization are the WTO agreements, which are the legal ground rules for international commerce. The agreements were negotiated and signed by most

关税及贸易总协定
General Agreement on Tariffs and Trade (GATT) a trade agreement, originally signed by 23 nations in 1947, that provided a forum for tariff negotiations and a place where international trade problems could be discussed and resolved

世界贸易组织
World Trade Organization (WTO) international organization dealing with the rules of trade between nations

Entrepreneurship in Action

Via Aviation: The Solution to an Industry Problem

Susan Mashibe
Business: Via Aviation
Founded: 2003, in Tanzania
Success: Via Aviation has achieved profitability in seven out of nine years.

A key to success for a new business is to address a widespread problem, and Tanzania-based Via Aviation does just that. Despite having 12 percent of the world population, Africa has less than 1 percent of the global air traffic market. Air travel in Africa can be inefficient and troublesome because of a lack of connecting flights, high fuel taxes, and a lack of ground services to replenish the aircraft for the next flight. Via Aviation addresses the problem by offering these ground services at various airports around Africa to facilitate more flights and increase efficiency. Founder Susan Mashibe's solution to this problem transformed air travel in Africa, not only by the establishment of these services, but also by accepting credit cards. Previously, pilots had to either pay for fuel in advance or carry thousands of dollars in cash with them in order to fuel their planes. Mashibe's contribution to the industry and her country has made her a reputable figure and earned her many awards and distinctions.[39]

---

of the world's trading nations and ratified by their parliaments. The goal is to help producers of goods and services and exporters and importers conduct their business. In addition to administering the WTO trade agreements, the WTO presents a forum for trade negotiations, monitors national trade policies, provides technical assistance and training for developing countries, and cooperates with other international organizations. Based in Geneva, Switzerland, the WTO has also adopted a leadership role in negotiating trade disputes among nations.[40] For example, Argentina filed a dispute with the WTO to protest anti-dumping measures instituted against them by the EU. The EU claimed Argentina was engaging in dumping biodiesel.[41]

北美自由贸易协定
The North American Free Trade Agreement

北美自由贸易协定
North American Free Trade Agreement (NAFTA)
agreement that eliminates most tariffs and trade restrictions on agricultural and manufactured products to encourage trade among Canada, the United States, and Mexico

The **North American Free Trade Agreement (NAFTA),** which went into effect on January 1, 1994, effectively merged Canada, the United States, and Mexico into one market of nearly 470 million consumers. NAFTA virtually eliminated all tariffs on goods produced and traded among Canada, Mexico, and the United States to create a free trade area. The estimated annual output for this trade alliance is about $17 trillion.[42] NAFTA makes it easier for U.S. businesses to invest in Mexico and Canada; provides protection for intellectual property (of special interest to high-technology and entertainment industries); expands trade by requiring equal treatment of U.S. firms in both countries; and simplifies country-of-origin rules, hindering Japan's use of Mexico as a staging ground for further penetration into U.S. markets.

Canada's nearly 35 million consumers are relatively affluent, with a per capita GDP of $43,100.[43] Trade between the United States and Canada totals approximately $680 billion.[44] About 79 percent of Canada's exports go to the United States, including mineral fuel and oil, vehicles, machinery, and plastic.[45] In fact, Canada is the single largest trading partner of the United States.[46]

With a per capita GDP of $15,600. Mexico's nearly 121 million consumers are less affluent than Canadian consumers.[47] However, trade with the United States and Mexico has tripled since NAFTA was initiated. Trade between the United States and Mexico totals more than $500 billion.[48] Millions of Americans cite their heritage as Mexican, making them the most populous Hispanic group in the country. These individuals often have close ties to relatives in Mexico and assist in Mexican–U.S. economic development and trade. Mexico is on a course of a market economy, rule of law, respect for human rights, and responsible public policies. There is also a commitment to the environment and sustainable human development. Many U.S. companies have taken advantage of Mexico's low labor costs and proximity to the United States to set up production facilities, sometimes called *maquiladoras.* Mexico is also attracting major technological industries, including electronics, software, and aerospace. Investors see many growth opportunities in Mexico, particularly in light of recent reforms. For instance, Mexico is considering legislation that would open up its state-controlled oil reserves to foreign companies. Additionally, if the United States does well economically, Mexico—its biggest customer—is also likely to do well.[49]

NAFTA, which went into effect on January 1, 1994, has increased trade among Mexico, the United States, and Canada.

However, there is great disparity within Mexico. The country's southern states cannot seem to catch up with the more affluent northern states on almost any socioeconomic indicator. The disparities are growing, as can be seen comparing the south to the northern industrial capital of Monterrey, which is beginning to seem like south Texas.[50] However, drug gang wars threaten the economic stability of Mexico, especially in the northern states close to the U.S. border. On the other hand, this situation is improving as the economy is growing and violence is decreasing.

Despite its benefits, NAFTA has been controversial, and disputes continue to arise over the implementation of the trade agreement. While many Americans feared the agreement would erase jobs in the United States, Mexicans have been disappointed that the agreement failed to create more jobs. Moreover, Mexico's rising standard of living has increased the cost of doing business there; many hundreds of *maquiladoras* have closed their doors and transferred work to other nations where labor costs are cheaper. Indeed, China has become the United States' second-largest importer.[51] On the other hand, high transportation costs, and the difficulty management often incurs in controlling a business so far away are now causing some manufacturers to reconsider opting for Mexican factories over China, even going so far as to relocate from China back to Mexico.[52]

Although NAFTA has been controversial, it has become a positive factor for U.S. firms wishing to engage in international marketing. Because licensing requirements have been relaxed under the pact, smaller businesses that previously could not afford to invest in Mexico and Canada will be able to do business in those markets without having to locate there. NAFTA's long phase-in period provided time for adjustment by those firms affected by reduced tariffs on imports. Furthermore, increased competition should lead to a more efficient market, and the long-term prospects of including most countries in the Western Hemisphere in the alliance promise additional opportunities for U.S. marketers.

欧洲联盟
The European Union

The **European Union (EU),** also called the *European Community* or *Common Market,* was established in 1958 to promote trade among its members, which initially included Belgium, France, Italy, West Germany, Luxembourg, and the Netherlands.

欧洲联盟
European Union (EU)
a union of European nations established in 1958 to promote trade among its members; one of the largest single markets today

East and West Germany united in 1991, and by 1995 the United Kingdom, Spain, Denmark, Greece, Portugal, Ireland, Austria, Finland, and Sweden had joined as well. The Czech Republic, Estonia, Hungary, Latvia, Lithuania, Poland, Slovakia, and Slovenia joined in 2004. In 2007, Bulgaria and Romania also became members, Cyprus and Malta joined in 2008, and Croatia joined in 2013, which brought total membership to 28. Macedonia, Iceland, and Turkey are candidate countries that hope to join the EU in the near future.[53] Until 1993, each nation functioned as a separate market, but at that time members officially unified into one of the largest single world markets, which today has nearly half a billion consumers with a GDP of more than $17 trillion.[54]

To facilitate free trade among members, the EU is working toward standardization of business regulations and requirements, import duties, and value-added taxes; the elimination of customs checks; and the creation of a standardized currency for use by all members. Many European nations (Austria, Belgium, Finland, France, Germany, Greece, Ireland, Italy, Luxembourg, the Netherlands, Portugal, Spain, and Slovenia) link their exchange rates to a common currency, the *euro;* however, several EU members have rejected use of the euro in their countries. Although the common currency requires many marketers to modify their pricing strategies and will subject them to increased competition, the use of a single currency frees companies that sell goods among European countries from the nuisance of dealing with complex exchange rates.[55] The long-term goals are to eliminate all trade barriers within the EU, improve the economic efficiency of the EU nations, and stimulate economic growth, thus making the union's economy more competitive in global markets, particularly against Japan and other Pacific Rim nations, and North America. However, several disputes and debates still divide the member nations, and many barriers to completely free trade remain. Consequently, it may take many years before the EU is truly one deregulated market.

The EU has also enacted some of the world's strictest laws concerning antitrust issues, which have had unexpected consequences for some non-European firms. For instance, European competition regulators have been investigating whether Google has been engaging in anticompetitive behavior since 2010. Google recently came to an agreement without admitting wrongdoing. To be more competitive, Google has agreed to display at least three of its rivals' postings along with its own for specialized searches. Google has stated it is also removing conditions that made it harder for its advertisers to move to competing sites.[56]

The Asia-Pacific Economic Cooperation (APEC) was established to promote open trade and cooperation among member nations.

The prosperity of the EU has suffered in recent years. EU members experienced a severe economic crisis in 2010 that required steep bailouts from the International Monetary Fund (IMF). The first country to come to the forefront was Greece, which had so much debt that it risked default. With an increase in Greek bond yields and credit risks—along with a severe deficit and other negative economic factors—the country's economy plummeted. Because Greece uses the euro as its currency, the massive downturn decreased the euro's value. This had a profound effect on other countries in the euro zone. (The euro zone refers collectively to European member countries that have adopted the euro as their form of currency.) Ireland and Portugal were particularly vulnerable because they had some of the region's largest deficits.[57] Ireland began experiencing problems similar to Greece, including a debt crisis, failing economic health, and rising bond yields.[58] Both Ireland and Portugal required bailout packages. In 2012, Spain and Cyprus also requested bailouts.

Greece continued to struggle even after the initial bailout because it did not have enough funds to repay its bondholders. Greece was forced to default. A default by one nation in the EU negatively affects the rest of the members by making them appear riskier as well.[59] In 2013, Standard & Poor's (S&P) downgraded the Netherlands from an AAA to an AA rating. As of 2013, only three countries in the euro zone—Finland, Germany, and Luxembourg—have maintained AAA ratings (the highest rating the S&P awards). Downgrades mean that the countries are perceived as riskier in terms of paying off their debt. Such downgrades could dissuade investors from investing in these countries.[60] Germany, on the other hand, has largely avoided the economic woes plaguing other countries. Germany has many exporting companies and has a smaller budget deficit and smaller household debt, which has enabled it to weather the crisis better than other EU members.[61]

亚太经济合作组织
Asia-Pacific Economic Cooperation

The **Asia-Pacific Economic Cooperation (APEC),** established in 1989, promotes open trade and economic and technical cooperation among member ecomonies, which initially included Australia, Brunei Darussalam, Canada, Indonesia, Japan, Korea, Malaysia, New Zealand, the Philippines, Singapore, Thailand, and the United States. Since then, the alliance has grown to include Chile; China; Hong Kong, China; Mexico; Papua New Guinea; Peru; Russia; Chinese Taipei; and Viet Nam. The 21-member alliance represents approximately 40 percent of the world's population, 44 percent of world trade, and 55 percent of world GDP. APEC differs from other international trade alliances in its commitment to facilitating business and its practice of allowing the business/private sector to participate in a wide range of APEC activities.[62]

亚太经济合作组织
Asia-Pacific Economic Cooperation (APEC)
an international trade alliance that promotes open trade and economic and technical cooperation among member nations

Companies of the APEC have become increasingly competitive and sophisticated in global business in the past three decades. The Japanese and South Koreans in particular have made tremendous inroads on world markets for automobiles, cameras, and audio and video equipment. Products from Samsung, Sony, Canon, Toyota, Daewoo, Mitsubishi, Suzuki, and Lenovo are sold all over the world and have set standards of quality by which other products are often judged. The People's Republic of China, a country of more than 1.3 billion people, has launched a program of economic reform to stimulate its economy by privatizing many industries, restructuring its banking system, and increasing public spending on infrastructure (including railways and telecommunications). As a result, China has become a manufacturing powerhouse, with an estimated economic growth rate of 7.7 percent a year.[63] China's export market has consistently outpaced its import growth in recent years and its GDP is the world's second-largest economy, behind the United States. In fact, China has overtaken the United States as the world's largest trader.[64]

Increased industrialization has also caused China to become the world's largest emitter of greenhouse gases in 2008. China has overtaken the United States to become the world's largest oil importer.[65] On the other hand, China has also begun a quest to become a world leader in green initiatives and renewable energy. This is an increasingly important quest as the country becomes more polluted.

Consider Ethics and Social Responsibility

Bangladesh Factory Disasters Prompt Better Safety Standards

Tragedies in Bangladesh are causing retailers to rethink how they approach worker safety in the factories from which they outsource. A fire at one Bangladesh factory killed 112 workers, and a building collapse at another factory killed more than 1,100 workers. In response many of the companies that use factories in Bangladesh are joining together with IndustriALL, a global federation of unions, to ensure safe working conditions. The proposal, crafted for the purposes of global agreement, requires that companies conduct and pay for safety inspections, publish the results, and have money set aside for any necessary renovations. These measures are estimated to cost each company about $500,000 per year.

Approximately 70 companies are included in the agreement, and it covers approximately 1,000 factories in Bangladesh. If a factory is found to have insufficient safety mechanisms, operations will be put on hold and workers will be sent home with pay until the repairs are made.

While this agreement was tailored for a global audience, many American companies are wary of joining the collaborative effort. Walmart and Gap are cautious because the agreement would make them vulnerable to unrestricted liability and potential lawsuits. Instead, the two companies are drafting their own set of safety standards to address unsafe factory conditions. While most of their initiatives are similar to those of the IndustriALL pact, they stop short of committing to financing necessary renovations. Supporters of the pact say that this last requirement is the enforceable part of the solution and that without it, there is no meaningful proposal.[66]

Discussion Questions

1. Why are suppliers finding the need to develop a global agreement improving worker safety conditions in Bangladesh?
2. Describe some ways that IndustriALL will improve worker safety.
3. Why are companies like Walmart and Gap developing their own supplier agreements?

Less visible Pacific Rim regions, such as Thailand, Singapore, Taiwan, Vietnam, and Hong Kong, have also become major manufacturing and financial centers. Vietnam, with one of the world's most open economies, has bypassed its communist government with private firms moving ahead despite bureaucracy, corruption, and poor infrastructure. In a country of 88 million, Vietnamese firms now compete internationally with an agricultural miracle, making the country one of the world's main providers of farm produce. Starbucks is expanding into Vietnam, with its first store in Ho Chi Minh City.[67]

东南亚国家联盟
Association of Southeast Asian Nations

东南亚国家联盟

Association of Southeast Asian Nations (ASEAN) A trade alliance that promotes trade and economic integration among member nations in Southeast Asia

The **Association of Southeast Asian Nations (ASEAN),** established in 1967, promotes trade and economic integration among member nations in Southeast Asia, including Malaysia, the Philippines, Singapore, Thailand, Brunei Darussalam, Vietnam, Laos, Indonesia, Myanmar, and Cambodia.[68] The 10-member alliance represents 600 million people with a GDP of $2 trillion.[69] ASEAN's goals include the promotion of free trade, peace, and collaboration between its members.[70]

In 1993, ASEAN began to reduce or phase out tariffs among countries and eliminate nontariff trade barriers.[71] This elimination of tariffs will encourage additional trade among countries and could be beneficial to businesses that want to export to other countries in the trading bloc.

However, ASEAN is facing challenges in becoming a unified trade bloc. Unlike members of the EU, the economic systems of ASEAN members are quite different, with political systems including dictatorships (Myanmar), democracies (Philippines and Malaysia), constitutional monarchies (Thailand and Cambodia), and communism (Vietnam).[72] Major conflicts have also occurred between member-nations.

Despite these challenges, ASEAN plans to increase economic integration by 2015, but unlike the EU, it will not have a common currency or fully free labor flows between member-nations. In this way, ASEAN plans to avoid some of the pitfalls that occurred among nations in the EU during the latest worldwide recession.[73]

Coffee is an important export for Panama.

世界银行
World Bank

The **World Bank,** more formally known as the International Bank for Reconstruction and Development, was established by the industrialized nations, including the United States, in 1946 to loan money to underdeveloped and developing countries.

It loans its own funds or borrows funds from member countries to finance projects ranging from road and factory construction to the building of medical and educational facilities. The World Bank and other multilateral development banks (banks with international support that provide loans to developing countries) are the largest source of advice and assistance for developing nations. The International Development Association and the International Finance Corporation are associated with the World Bank and provide loans to private businesses and member countries.

世界银行
World Bank
an organization established by the industrialized nations in 1946 to loan money to underdeveloped and developing countries; formally known as the International Bank for Reconstruction and Development

国际货币基金组织
International Monetary Fund

The **International Monetary Fund (IMF)** was established in 1947 to promote trade among member nations by eliminating trade barriers and fostering financial cooperation. It also makes short-term loans to member countries that have balance-of-payment deficits and provides foreign currencies to member nations. The IMF tries to avoid financial crises and panics by alerting the international community about countries that will not be able to repay their debts. The IMF's Internet site provides additional information about the organization, including news releases, frequently asked questions, and members.

The IMF is the closest thing the world has to an international central bank. If countries get into financial trouble, they can borrow from the World Bank. However, the global economic crisis created many challenges for the IMF as it was forced to significantly increase its loans to both emerging economies and more developed nations. The usefulness of the IMF for developed countries is limited because these countries use private markets as a major source of capital.[74] Yet the European debt crisis changed this somewhat. Portugal, Ireland, Greece, and Spain (often referred to with the acronym PIGS) required billions of dollars in bailouts from the IMF to keep their economies afloat.

国际货币基金组织
International Monetary Fund (IMF)
organization established in 1947 to promote trade among member nations by eliminating trade barriers and fostering financial cooperation

LO 3-4

参与国际商务
Getting Involved in International Business

Businesses may get involved in international trade at many levels—from a small Kenyan firm that occasionally exports African crafts to a huge multinational corporation such as Shell Oil that sells products around the globe. The degree of commitment of resources and effort required increases according to the level at which a business involves itself in international trade. This section examines exporting and importing, trading companies, licensing and franchising, contract manufacturing, joint ventures, direct investment, and multinational corporations.

出口和进口
Exporting and Importing

Many companies first get involved in international trade when they import goods from other countries for resale in their own businesses. For example, a grocery store chain may import bananas from Honduras and coffee from Colombia. A business may get involved in exporting when it is called upon to supply a foreign company with a particular product. Such exporting enables enterprises of all sizes to participate in international business. Exporting to other countries becomes a necessity for established countries that seek to grow continually. Products often have higher sales growth potential in foreign countries than they have in the parent country. For instance, General Motors and YUM Brands! sell more of their products in China than in the United States. Walmart experienced sales growth in international markets. Figure 3.2 shows some of the world's largest exporting countries.

对销贸易协定
countertrade agreements
foreign trade agreements that involve bartering products for other products instead of for currency

Exporting sometimes takes place through **countertrade agreements,** which involve bartering products for other products instead of for currency. Such arrangements are fairly common in international trade, especially between Western companies and eastern European nations. An estimated 40 percent or more of all international trade agreements contain countertrade provisions.

FIGURE 3.2
Top Exporting Countries

Source: "Country Comparison: Exports," *The CIA World Facebook.*

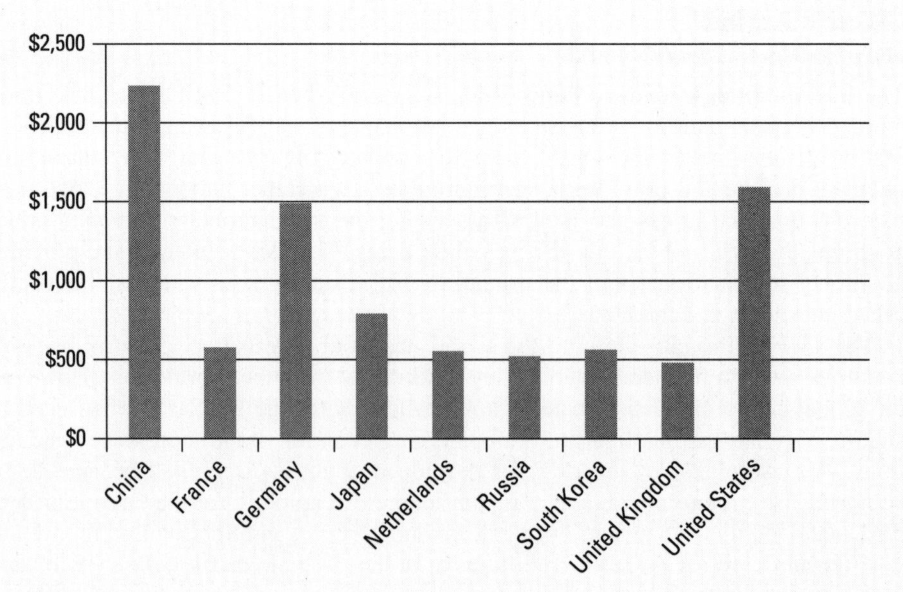

Although a company may export its wares overseas directly or import goods directly from their manufacturer, many choose to deal with an intermediary, commonly called an *export agent.* Export agents seldom produce goods themselves; instead, they usually handle international transactions for other firms. Export agents either purchase products outright or take them on consignment. If they purchase them outright, they generally mark up the price they have paid and attempt to sell the product in the international marketplace. They are also responsible for storage and transportation.

An advantage of trading through an agent instead of directly is that the company does not have to deal with foreign currencies or the red tape (paying tariffs and handling paperwork) of international business. A major disadvantage is that, because the export agent must make a profit, either the price of the product must be increased or the domestic company must provide a larger discount than it would in a domestic transaction.

贸易公司
Trading Companies

A **trading company** buys goods in one country and sells them to buyers in another country. Trading companies handle all activities required to move products from one country to another, including consulting, marketing research, advertising, insurance, product research and design, warehousing, and foreign exchange services to companies interested in selling their products in foreign markets. Trading companies are similar to export agents, but their role in international trade is larger. By linking sellers and buyers of goods in different countries, trading companies promote international trade. The best-known U.S. trading company is Sears World Trade, which specializes in consumer goods, light industrial items, and processed foods.

贸易公司
trading company
a firm that buys goods in one country and sells them to buyers in another country

授权与特许经营
Licensing and Franchising

Licensing is a trade arrangement in which one company—the *licensor*—allows another company—the *licensee*—to use its company name, products, patents, brands, trademarks, raw materials, and/or production processes in exchange for a fee or royalty. The Coca-Cola Company and PepsiCo frequently use licensing as a means to market their soft drinks, apparel, and other merchandise in other countries. Licensing is an attractive alternative to direct investment when the political stability of a foreign country is in doubt or when resources are unavailable for direct investment. Licensing is especially advantageous for small manufacturers wanting to launch a well-known brand internationally. Yoplait is a French yogurt that is licensed for production in the United States.

授权
licensing
a trade agreement in which one company—the licensor—allows another company—the licensee—to use its company name, products, patents, brands, trademarks, raw materials, and/or production processes in exchange for a fee or royalty

Franchising is a form of licensing in which a company—the *franchiser*—agrees to provide a *franchisee* the name, logo, methods of operation, advertising, products, and other elements associated with the franchiser's business, in return for a financial commitment and the agreement to conduct business in accordance with the franchiser's standard of operations. Wendy's, McDonald's, H&R Block, and Holiday Inn are well-known franchisers with international visibility. Table 3.4 lists some of the top global franchises.

特许经营
franchising
a form of licensing in which a company—the franchiser—agrees to provide a franchisee a name, logo, methods of operation, advertising, products, and other elements associated with a franchiser's business in return for a financial commitment and the agreement to conduct business in accordance with the franchiser's standard of operations

Licensing and franchising enable a company to enter the international marketplace without spending large sums of money abroad or hiring or transferring personnel to handle overseas affairs. They also minimize problems associated with shipping costs, tariffs, and trade restrictions, and they allow the firm to establish goodwill for its products in a foreign market, which will help the company if it decides to produce or market its products directly in the foreign country at some future date. However, if the licensee (or franchisee) does not maintain high standards of quality, the product's image may be hurt; therefore, it is important for the licensor to monitor its products overseas and to enforce its quality standards.

TABLE 3.4
Top Global Franchises

Franchise	Country	Ranking
Subway	United States	1
McDonald's	United States	2
DIA	Spain	10
InterContinental Hotels Group	United Kingdom	15
Groupe Casino	France	29
Tim Hortons	Canada	32
Kumon North America Inc.	Japan	43
Husse	Sweden	61
Cartridge World	Australia	79
Five Guys Burgers and Fries	United States	99

Source: "Top 100 Global Franchises—Rankings," Franchise Direct.

合同制造
contract manufacturing the hiring of a foreign company to produce a specified volume of the initiating company's product to specification; the final product carries the domestic firm's name

合同制造
Contract Manufacturing

Contract manufacturing occurs when a company hires a foreign company to produce a specified volume of the firm's product to specification; the final product carries the domestic firm's name. Spalding, for example, relies on contract manufacturing for its sports equipment; Reebok uses Korean contract manufacturers to manufacture many of its athletic shoes.

外包
Outsourcing

Earlier, we defined outsourcing as transferring manufacturing or other tasks (such as information technology operations) to companies in countries where labor and supplies are less expensive. Many U.S. firms have outsourced tasks to India, Ireland, Mexico, and the Philippines, where there are many well-educated workers and significantly lower labor costs. Services, such as taxes or customer service, can also be outsourced.

Although outsourcing has become politically controversial in recent years amid concerns over jobs lost to overseas workers, foreign companies transfer tasks and jobs to U.S. companies—sometimes called *insourcing*—far more often than U.S. companies outsource tasks and jobs abroad.[75] However, some firms are bringing their outsourced jobs back after concerns that foreign workers were not adding enough value. Companies such as General Electric and Caterpillar are returning to the United States due to increasing labor costs in some places, the expense of shipping products across the ocean, and fears of fraud or intellectual property theft. Companies from other countries have also been moving some of their production to the United States; Chinese computer-maker Lenovo is opening a production facility in the United States. Apple also announced it would start building a line of Mac computers in America.[76]

离岸外包
offshoring the relocation of business processes by a company or subsidiary to another country; offshoring is different than outsourcing because the company retains control of the offshored processes

离岸外包
Offshoring

Offshoring is the relocation of a business process by a company, or a subsidiary, to another country. Offshoring is different than outsourcing: the company retains control of the process because it is not subcontracting to a different company. Companies may choose to offshore for a number of reasons, ranging from lower wages, skilled labor, or taking advantage of time zone differences in order to offer services around the clock. Some banks have chosen not to outsource because of concerns about data security in other countries. These institutions may instead engage in offshoring, which allows a company more control over international operations because the offshore office is an extension of the company. Barclays Bank, for instance, has an international offshore banking unit called Barclays Wealth International. This branch helps the company better serve wealthy clients with international banking needs.[77]

This Subway restaurant is part of the huge Souq Sharq shopping center in Kuwait City, Kuwait.

合资企业与联盟
Joint Ventures and Alliances

Many countries, particularly LDCs, do not permit direct investment by foreign companies or individuals. A company may also lack sufficient resources or expertise to operate in another country. In such cases, a company that wants to do business in another country may set up a **joint venture** by finding a local partner (occasionally, the host nation itself) to share the costs and operation of the business. General Motors has been able to break into the Chinese market by partnering with local companies. During the 1990s, GM formed a joint venture with state-owned SAIC Motor to form Shanghai General Motors Company. It currently operates 12 joint ventures in China.[78]

合资企业
joint venture the sharing of the costs and operation of a business between a foreign company and a local partner

In some industries, such as automobiles and computers, strategic alliances are becoming the predominant means of competing. A **strategic alliance** is a partnership formed to create competitive advantage on a worldwide basis. In such industries, international competition is so fierce and the costs of competing on a global basis are so high that few firms have the resources to go it alone, so they collaborate with other companies. An example of a strategic alliance is the partnership between Polish bank PKO Bank Polski and payments service provider EVO Payments International LLC. The two companies embarked upon a 20-year strategic alliance. As part of the partnership, EVO acquired a 66 percent stake in PKO's merchant acquiring service eService. Over the duration of the partnership, the two companies will work to develop eService into a leading merchant acquirer.[79]

战略联盟
strategic alliance a partnership formed to create competitive advantage on a worldwide basis

直接投资
Direct Investment

Companies that want more control and are willing to invest considerable resources in international business may consider **direct investment,** the ownership of overseas facilities. Direct investment may involve the development and operation of new facilities—such as when Starbucks opens a new coffee shop in Japan—or the purchase of all or part of an existing operation in a foreign country. Nokia acquired its partner Siemens' 50 percent stake in their joint venture Nokia Siemens Networks. Nokia Siemens Networks became a wholly owned subsidiary of Nokia after the firm paid Siemens 1.7 billion euros for the stake.[80]

直接投资
direct investment the ownership of overseas facilities

The highest level of international business involvement is the **multinational corporation (MNC),** a corporation, such as IBM or ExxonMobil, that operates on a worldwide scale, without significant ties to any one nation or region. Table 3.5 lists 10 well-known

跨国公司
multinational corporation (MNC) a corporation that operates on a worldwide scale, without significant ties to any one nation or region

Walmart has chosen to invest directly in China. However, it must still make adjustments to fit with the local culture. For instance, Walmart was pressured to allow Chinese employees to unionize.

multinational corporations. MNCs are more than simple corporations. They often have greater assets than some of the countries in which they do business. Nestlé, with headquarters in Switzerland, operates more than 400 factories around the world and receives revenues from Europe; North, Central, and South America; Africa; and Asia.[81] The Royal Dutch/Shell Group, one of the world's major oil producers, is another MNC. Its main offices are located in The Hague and London. Other MNCs include BASF, British Petroleum, Matsushita, Mitsubishi, Siemens, Texaco, Toyota, and Unilever. Many MNCs have been targeted by antiglobalization activists at global business forums, and some protests have turned violent. The activists contend that MNCs increase the gap between rich and poor nations, misuse and misallocate scarce resources, exploit the labor markets in LDCs, and harm their natural environments.[82]

国际商务战略
International Business Strategies

Planning in a global economy requires businesspeople to understand the economic, legal, political, and sociocultural realities of the countries in which they will operate. These factors will affect the strategy a business chooses to use outside its own borders.

TABLE 3.5
Large Multinational Companies

Company	Country	Description
Royal Dutch Shell	Netherlands	Oil and gas; largest company in the world in terms of revenue
Toyota	Japan	Largest automobile manufacturer in the world
Walmart	United States	Largest retailer in the world; largest private employer in the world
Siemens	Germany	Engineering and electronics; largest engineering company in Europe
Nestlé	Switzerland	Nutritional, snack-food, and health-related consumer goods
Samsung	South Korea	Subsidiaries specializing in electronics, electronic components, telecommunications equipment, medical equipment, and more
Unilever	United Kingdom	Consumer goods including cleaning and personal care, foods, beverages
Boeing	United States	Aerospace and defense; largest U.S. exporter
Lenovo	China	Computer technology; highest share of PC market
Subway	United States	Largest fast-food chain; fastest growing franchises in 105 countries

发展战略
Developing Strategies

Companies doing business internationally have traditionally used a **multinational strategy,** customizing their products, promotion, and distribution according to cultural, technological, regional, and national differences. McDonald's recently opened its first restaurant in Vietnam. While it will offer its usual menu, McDonald's also recognizes that Vietamese consumers have their own preferences. In addition to its usual offerings, McDonald's Vietnam is also offering McPork sandwiches specifically targeted toward Vientnam consumers.[83] Many soap and detergent manufacturers have adapted their products to local water conditions, washing equipment, and washing habits. For customers in some LDCs, Colgate-Palmolive Co. has developed an inexpensive, plastic, hand-powered washing machine for use in households that have no electricity. Even when products are standardized, advertising often has to be modified to adapt to language and cultural differences. Also, celebrities used in advertising in the United States may be unfamiliar to foreign consumers and thus would not be effective in advertising products in other countries.

多国战略
multinational strategy
a plan, used by international companies, that involves customizing products, promotion, and distribution according to cultural, technological, regional, and national differences

More and more companies are moving from this customization strategy to a **global strategy (globalization),** which involves standardizing products (and, as much as possible, their promotion and distribution) for the whole world, as if it were a single entity. Examples of globalized products are American clothing, movies, music, and cosmetics. As it has become a global brand, Starbucks has standardized its products and stores. Starbucks was ranked as one of the world's most engaged brands in terms of online activities, even surpassing Coca-Cola, which is another global brand.

全球战略
global strategy (globalization)
a strategy that involves standardizing products (and, as much as possible, their promotion and distribution) for the whole world, as if it were a single entity

Before moving outside their own borders, companies must conduct environmental analyses to evaluate the potential of and problems associated with various markets and to determine what strategy is best for doing business in those markets. Failure to do so may result in losses and even negative publicity. Some companies rely on local managers to gain greater insights and faster response to changes within a country. Astute businesspeople today "think globally, act locally." That is, while constantly being aware of the total picture, they adjust their firms' strategies to conform to local needs and tastes.

管理全球商业挑战
Managing the Challenges of Global Business

As we've pointed out in this chapter, many past political barriers to trade have fallen or been minimized, expanding and opening new market opportunities. Managers who can meet the challenges of creating and implementing effective and sensitive business strategies for the global marketplace can help lead their companies to success. For example, the Commercial Service is the global business solutions unit of the U.S. Department of Commerce that offers U.S. firms wide and deep practical knowledge of international markets and industries, a unique global network, inventive use of information technology, and a focus on small and mid-sized businesses. Another example is the benchmarking of best international practices that benefits U.S. firms, which is conducted by the network of CIBERs (Centers for International Business Education and Research) at leading business schools in the United States. These CIBERs are funded by the U.S. government to help U.S. firms become more competitive globally. A major element of the assistance that these governmental organizations can provide firms (especially for small and medium-sized firms) is knowledge of the internationalization process.[84] Small businesses, too, can succeed in foreign markets when their managers have carefully studied those markets and prepared and implemented appropriate strategies. Being globally aware is therefore an important quality for today's managers and will become a critical attribute for managers of the 21st century.

So You Want a Job in Global Business

Have you always dreamt of traveling the world? Whether backpacking your way through Central America or sipping espressos at five-star European restaurants is your style, the increasing globalization of business might just give you your chance to see what the world has to offer. Most new jobs will have at least some global component, even if located within the United States, so being globally aware and keeping an open mind to different cultures is vital in today's business world. Think about the 1.3 billion consumers in China that have already purchased 500 million mobile phones. In the future, some of the largest markets will be in Asia.

As more and more companies sell products around the globe, their function, design, packaging, and promotions need to be culturally relevant to many different people in many different places. Products very often cross multiple borders before reaching the final consumer, both in their distribution and through the supply chain to produce the products.

Jobs exist in export and import management, product and pricing management, distribution and transportation, and advertising. Many "born global" companies such as Google operate virtually and consider all countries their market. Many companies sell their products through eBay and other Internet sites and never leave the United States. Today communication and transportation facilitates selling and buying products worldwide with delivery in a few days. You may have sold or purchased a product on eBay outside the United States without thinking about how easy and accessible international markets are to business. If you have, welcome to the world of global business.

To be successful you must have an idea not only of differing regulations from country to country, but of different language, ethics, and communication styles and varying needs and wants of international markets. From a regulatory side, you may need to be aware of laws related to intellectual property, copyrights, antitrust, advertising, and pricing in every country. Translating is never only about translating the language. Perhaps even more important is ensuring that your message gets through. Whether on a product label or in advertising or promotional materials, the use of images and words varies widely across the globe.

Review Your Understanding

Explore some of the factors within the international trade environment that influence business.

International business is the buying, selling, and trading of goods and services across national boundaries. Importing is the purchase of products and raw materials from another nation; exporting is the sale of domestic goods and materials to another nation. A nation's balance of trade is the difference in value between its exports and imports; a negative balance of trade is a trade deficit. The difference between the flow of money into a country and the flow of money out of it is called the balance of payments. An absolute or comparative advantage in trade may determine what products a company from a particular nation will export.

Investigate some of the economic, legal, political, social, cultural, and technological barriers to international business.

Companies engaged in international trade must consider the effects of economic, legal, political, social, and cultural differences between nations. Economic barriers are a country's level of development (infrastructure) and exchange rates. Wide-ranging legal and political barriers include differing laws (and enforcement), tariffs, exchange controls, quotas, embargoes, political instability, and war. Ambiguous cultural and social barriers involve differences in spoken and body language, time, holidays and other observances, and customs.

Specify some of the agreements, alliances, and organizations that may encourage trade across international boundaries.

Among the most important promoters of international business are the General Agreement on Tariffs and Trade, the World Trade Organization, the North American Free Trade Agreement, the European Union, the Asia-Pacific Economic Cooperation, the Association of Southeast Asian Nations, the World Bank, and the International Monetary Fund.

Summarize the different levels of organizational involvement in international trade.

A company may be involved in international trade at several levels, each requiring a greater commitment of resources and effort, ranging from importing/exporting to multinational corporations. Countertrade agreements occur at the import/export level and involve bartering products for other products instead of currency. At the next level, a trading company links buyers and sellers in different countries to foster trade. In licensing and franchising, one company agrees to allow a foreign company the use of its company name, products, patents, brands, trademarks, raw materials, and production processes in exchange for a flat fee or royalty. Contract manufacturing occurs when a company hires a foreign company to produce a specified volume of the firm's product to specification; the final product carries the domestic firm's name. A joint venture is a partnership in which companies from different countries agree to share the costs and operation of the business. The purchase of overseas production and marketing facilities is direct investment. Outsourcing, a form of direct investment, involves transferring manufacturing to countries where labor and supplies are cheap. Offshoring is the relocation of business processes by a company or subsidiary to another country; it differs from outsourcing because the company retains control of the offshored processes. A multinational corporation is one that operates on a worldwide scale, without significant ties to any one nation or region.

Contrast two basic strategies used in international business.

Companies typically use one of two basic strategies in international business. A multinational strategy customizes products, promotion, and distribution according to cultural, technological, regional, and national differences. A global strategy (globalization) standardizes products (and, as much as possible, their promotion and distribution) for the whole world, as if it were a single entity.

Assess the opportunities and problems facing a small business that is considering expanding into international markets.

"Solve the Dilemma" on page 111 presents a small business considering expansion into international markets. Based on the material provided in the chapter, analyze the business's position, evaluating specific markets, anticipating problems, and exploring methods of international involvement.

Revisit the World of Business

1. Why does Xiaomi appeal to the average Chinese consumer?
2. Why might Xiaomi's cool, hip image in China be tarnished if it goes global?
3. Describe the barriers Xiaomi will likely face as it expands into the United States.

Learn the Terms

absolute advantage
Asia-Pacific Economic Cooperation (APEC)
Association of Southeast Asian Nations (ASEAN)
balance of payments
balance of trade
cartel
comparative advantage
contract manufacturing
countertrade agreements
direct investment
dumping
embargo
European Union (EU)
exchange controls
exchange rate
exporting
franchising
General Agreement on Tariffs and Trade (GATT)
global strategy (globalization)
import tariff
importing
infrastructure
international business
International Monetary Fund (IMF)
joint venture
licensing
multinational corporation (MNC)
multinational strategy
North American Free Trade Agreement (NAFTA)
offshoring
outsourcing
quota
strategic alliance
trade deficit
trading company
World Bank
World Trade Organization (WTO)

Check Your Progress

1. Distinguish between an absolute advantage and a comparative advantage. Cite an example of a country that has an absolute advantage and one with a comparative advantage.
2. What effect does devaluation have on a nation's currency? Can you think of a country that has devalued or revaluated its currency? What have been the results?
3. What effect does a country's economic development have on international business?
4. How do political issues affect international business?
5. What is an import tariff? A quota? Dumping? How might a country use import tariffs and quotas to control its balance of trade and payments? Why can dumping result in the imposition of tariffs and quotas?
6. How do social and cultural differences create barriers to international trade? Can you think of any additional social or cultural barriers (other than those mentioned in this chapter) that might inhibit international business?

7. Explain how a countertrade agreement can be considered a trade promoter. How does the World Trade Organization encourage trade?
8. At what levels might a firm get involved in international business? What level requires the least commitment of resources? What level requires the most?
9. Compare and contrast licensing, franchising, contract manufacturing, and outsourcing.
10. Compare multinational and global strategies. Which is better? Under what circumstances might each be used?

Get Involved

1. If the United States were to impose additional tariffs on cars imported from Japan, what would happen to the price of Japanese cars sold in the United States? What would happen to the price of American cars? What action might Japan take to continue to compete in the U.S. automobile market?
2. Although NAFTA has been controversial, it has been a positive factor for U.S. firms desiring to engage in international business. What industries and specific companies have the greatest potential for opening stores in Canada and Mexico? What opportunities exist for small businesses that cannot afford direct investment in Mexico and Canada?
3. Identify a local company that is active in international trade. What is its level of international business involvement and why? Analyze the threats and opportunities it faces in foreign markets, as well as its strengths and weaknesses in meeting those challenges. Based on your analysis, make some recommendations for the business's future involvement in international trade. (Your instructor may ask you to share your report with the class.)

Build Your Skills

Global Awareness

Background

As American businesspeople travel the globe, they encounter and must quickly adapt to a variety of cultural norms quite different from the United States. When encountering individuals from other parts of the world, the best attitude to adopt is "Here is my way. Now what is yours?" The more you see that you are part of a complex world and that your culture is different from, not better than, others, the better you will communicate and the more effective you will be in a variety of situations. It takes time, energy, understanding, and tolerance to learn about and appreciate other cultures. Naturally you're more comfortable doing things the way you've always done them. Remember, however, that this fact will also be true of the people from other cultures with whom you are doing business.

Task

You will "travel the globe" by answering questions related to some of the cultural norms that are found in other countries. Form groups of four to six class members and determine the answers to the following questions. Your instructor has the answer key, which will allow you to determine your group's Global Awareness IQ, which is based on a maximum score of 100 points (10 points per question).

Match the country with the cultural descriptor provided.

A. Saudi Arabia **F.** China
B. Japan **G.** Greece
C. Great Britain **H.** Korea
D. Germany **I.** India
E. Venezuela **J.** Mexico

_____ **1.** When people in this country table a motion, they want to discuss it. In America, "to table a motion" means to put off discussion.

_____ **2.** In this country, special forms of speech called *keigo* convey status among speakers. When talking with a person in this country, one should know the person's rank. People from this country will not initiate a conversation without a formal introduction.

_____ **3.** People from this country pride themselves on enhancing their image by keeping others waiting.

_____ **4.** When writing a business letter, people in this country like to provide a great deal of background information and detail before presenting their main points.

_____ **5.** For a man to inquire about another man's wife (even a general question about how she is doing) is considered very offensive in this country.

_____ **6.** When in this country, you are expected to negotiate the price on goods you wish to purchase.

_____ **7.** While North Americans want to decide the main points at a business meeting and leave the details for later, people in this country need to have all details decided before the meeting ends to avoid suspicion and distrust.

_____ **8.** Children in this country learn from a very early age to look down respectfully when talking to those of higher status.

_____ **9.** In this country the husband is the ruler of the household, and the custom is to keep the women hidden.

_____ **10.** Many businesspeople from the United States experience frustration because yes does not always mean the same thing in other cultures. For example, the word *yes* in this country means, "OK, I want to respect you and not offend you." It does not necessarily show agreement.

Solve the Dilemma

Global Expansion or Business as Usual?

Audiotech Electronics, founded in 1959 by a father and son, currently operates a 35,000-square-foot factory with 75 employees. The company produces control consoles for television and radio stations and recording studios. It is involved in every facet of production—designing the systems, installing the circuits in its computer boards, and even manufacturing and painting the metal cases housing the consoles. The company's products are used by all the major broadcast and cable networks. The firm's newest products allow television correspondents to simultaneously hear and communicate with their counterparts in different geographic locations. Audiotech has been very successful meeting its customers' needs efficiently.

Audiotech sales have historically been strong in the United States, but recently, growth is stagnating. Even though Audiotech is a small, family-owned firm, it believes it should evaluate and consider global expansion.

Discussion Questions

1. What are the key issues that need to be considered in determining global expansion?
2. What are some of the unique problems that a small business might face in global expansion that larger firms would not?
3. Should Audiotech consider a joint venture? Should it hire a sales force of people native to the countries it enters?

Build Your Business Plan

Business in a Borderless World

Think about the good/service you are contemplating for your business plan. If it is an already established good or service, try to find out if the product is currently being sold internationally. If not, can you identify opportunities to do so in the future? What countries do you think would respond most favorably to your product? What problems would you encounter if you attempted to export your product to those countries?

If you are thinking of creating a new good or service for your business plan, think about the possibility of eventually marketing that product in another country. What countries or areas of the world do you think would be most responsive to your product?

Are there countries the United States has trade agreements or alliances with that would make your entry into the market easier? What would be the economic, social, cultural, and technological barriers you would have to recognize before entering the prospective country(ies)? Think about the specific cultural differences that would have to be taken into consideration before entering the prospective country.

See for Yourself Videocase

Walt Disney around the Globe

Mickey Mouse has been a beloved American icon since the 1930s. The success of this and other Disney characters helped to build Disney theme parks; first in Anaheim, California, in 1955 and then in Orlando, Florida, 16 years later. For decades, tourists from all over the globe traveled in droves to California or Florida to experience the "happiest place on earth." What could be more natural for Disney than to introduce Mickey around the globe with international parks?

Disneyland first opened on the international front in Tokyo, Japan, in 1983. Ten years later, Disney brought the magic to Paris, France. Finally, in 2005, Disneyland opened its gates in Hong Kong, China. Global expansion is tricky for any business. There are many challenges to overcome, such as economic, legal, political, social, and cultural barriers. While Mickey may be recognized and loved around the world, this does not mean that duplicating American parks in other countries will be a success.

Perhaps the greatest challenge for Disney when entering new international markets has been how to handle cultural differences. Euro Disney (later renamed Disneyland Resort Paris) opened near Paris, France, in 1992 to fanfare and problems. Many well-known French citizens and labor unions vocally opposed the park because they felt that it was wrong to allow a symbol of American culture to become a focal point in France. Attendance for the first three years was well below expectations, causing grave financial difficulties. Finally, in 1995, the park experienced a turnaround. Financial restructuring helped the park achieve profitability. New attractions, lower admission prices, renaming the park as Disneyland Paris, and a marketing campaign increased attendance. The park, now the number-one tourist attraction in Europe with nearly 15 million visitors per year, continues to expand in anticipation of future growth. The theme park has attracted more than 250 million visitors in its 20-year history.

Having learned from its experience in France, The Walt Disney Company entered its venture in Hong Kong with an eye to embracing and honoring local culture. The company had learned to be sensitive to cultural variations in events, trends, and cuisine. The parks must embrace local culture while staying true to the Disney message. To this end, Disney hired a feng shui consultant to assist with the layout of the Hong Kong park. The fourth floor was eliminated at all hotels because of the cultural belief that the number four is bad luck. One of the Hong Kong Disneyland ballrooms measures 888 square meters because eight signifies wealth in Chinese culture. Even with this attention to detail, Hong Kong Disneyland's first years have been rough, with attendance far below projections and protestors raising cultural and social objections. A major complaint among guests has been that the park is small. Over the next decade, the company plans to invest half a billion dollars in expansion efforts. Disney is also building another theme park in Shanghai, China. This park will be two to three times as large as Hong Kong Disney and is set to be completed in 2016.

While some locals continue to protest Disney's presence, there are benefits to allowing a global company like Disney to enter foreign markets. Disney theme parks attract both local and global tourists, which can be a major stimulus to the local economy. For example, Hong Kong expects that Hong Kong Disneyland will bring more than 50,000 jobs to the city between 2005 and 2025. Experts predict that the park will bring $19 billion (U.S.) to the local economy during the park's first 40 years. It is likely that, with expansion and further refinement, Hong Kong Disneyland will be a success in the long run. Problems in France and Hong Kong have not deterred The Walt Disney Company from further global expansion. Hopefully, the company has learned that it must pay close attention to cultural and social variances in global markets in order to succeed.[87]

Discussion Questions

1. What led The Walt Disney Company to believe that its theme parks would be successful internationally?
2. What stumbling blocks did Disney encounter at their France and Hong Kong theme parks?
3. What are some of the factors complicating international expansion of a brand like Disney? What can a multinational corporation do to mitigate these issues?

You can find the related video in the Video Library in Connect. Ask your instructor how you can access Connect.

Notes 注释

Chapter 1

1. Travis Hoium, "Coke and Pepsi Up Against a Young Monster, and Losing," *Daily Finance*, March 26, 2013; Geoff Colvin, "The 50 Greatest Business Rivalries of All Time—A Little Competition," *Fortune*, March 21, 2013; Kim Bhasin, "Coke vs. Pepsi: The Amazing Story Behind the Cola Wars," *Business Insider*, November 2, 2011; Anastasia Kourovskaia, "Soft Drink Top 2013," *Kantar UK Insights*, June 28, 2013.
2. "Diversity Resources," The Graduate Management Admissions Council.
3. Philip Fava, "Recycling E-Waste: How One Company Gets It Right," *Forbes*, November 13, 2012.
4. Loretta Chao, "As Rivals Outsource, Lenovo Keeps Production In-House," *The Wall Street Journal*, July 9, 2012.
5. Serena Ng, "Soap Opera: Amazon Moves In With P&G," *The Wall Street Journal*, October 15, 2013, pp. A1 and A2.
6. Caleb Melby, "Hershey Invests $300 Million in Future of American Manufacturing . . . and Consumption," *Forbes*, September 25, 2012.
7. Michael McCutcheon, "How Millennials Are Responding to Coca Cola's New Anti-Obesity Campaign," *Policy Mic*, January 16, 2013; Steven Reinberg, "Food Companies Cut 6.4 Trillion Calories from Supermarket Shelves: Report," *Health Day*, January 9, 2014.
8. "Got Milk?".
9. "About Bill Daniels," .
10. "Special Report: The Visible Hand."
11. "The Shark Tank," *ABC*.
12. "World Ranking 2013 of Hotel Groups and Brands," Hospitality.net, April 3, 2013; Dan Schawbel, "J.W. Marriott Jr: From Root Beer Stand to Global Hotel Company," *Forbes*, February 4, 2013; "Marriott Gets Small to Go Big," *Fortune*, February 24, 2014, p. 14.
13. The Economist, "Swiss Watchmakers: Time Is Money," *The Economist*, February 16, 2013; James Shotter, "Swiss Regulator Winds Back on Swatch Deal," *Financial Times*, July 12, 2013; Thomas Mulier, "Swatch Allowed to Cut Only Movement Sales, Regulator Says," *Bloomberg*, July 12, 2013.
14. World International Property Organization, "International Patent Filings Set New Record in 2011," March 5, 2012.
15. Paul Toscano, "The Worst Hyperinfl ation Situations of All Time," *CNBC*, February 14, 2011.
16. "Zimbabwe," CIA—*The World Factbook*.
17. Stephan Dinan, "U.S. Debt Jumps a Record $328 Billion—Tops $17 Trillion for the First Time," *Washington Times*, October 18, 2013.
18. Chris Woodyard, "If a Tree Falls in the Forest, Does It End Up in a Car?" *USA Today*, June 28, 2013, p. 3B; Bill Esler, "Real Wood Preferred in Eco Car Interiors," Wood Working Network, July 8, 2013; Ford, "Ford Uses Kenaf Plant Inside Doors in the All-New Escape, Saving Weight and Energy".
19. U.S. Census Bureau, "State & County Quick Facts"; Haya El Nasser, Gregory Korte, and Paul Overberg, "308.7 Million," *USA Today*, December 22, 2010, p. 1A.
20. Liz Peek, "Why Women Are Leaving the Workforce in Record Numbers," *The Fiscal Times*, April 17, 2013.
21. Telis Demos and Ian Sherr, "IPO Action for GoPro Camera Maker," *The Wall Street Journal*, February 8–9, 2014, p. B3.
22. Eli Lilly, "Heritage".
23. Emeco, "About Emeco," Emeco website; CBS News, "Exploring the History of An Iconic Chair," *CBS*, January 6, 2014; Christopher Jon Sprigman and Kal Raustiala, "Can Restoration Hardware Legally Knockoff the Navy Chair?" *Slate*, November 26, 2012.
24. Walmart, "Corporate and Financial Facts," February 2014; Anthony Bianco and Wendy Zellner, "Is Wal-Mart Too Powerful?" *BusinessWeek*, October 6, 2003, pp. 100–10.
25. "Stopping SOPA," *The Economist*, January 21, 2012, p. 33.
26. "The 2011 World's Most Ethical Companies," *Ethisphere*, 2011, Q1, pp. 37–43.
27. Isabelle Maignon, Tracy L. Gonzalez-Padron, G. Tomas M. Hult, and O. C. Ferrell, "Stakeholder Orientation: Development and Testing of a Framework for Socially Responsible Marketing," *Journal of Strategic Marketing*, 19, no. 4 (July 2011), pp. 313–338.
28. Small Business Administration Office of Advocacy, *Frequently Asked Questions*, 2012; Joel Holland, "Save the World, Make a Million," *Entrepreneur*, April 2010; iContact.
29. Kevin Kelleher, "The Rise of Redbox Should Spook Netfl ix," *CNNMoney*, February 10, 2012; Marc Graser, "Redbox Now Controls More than 50% of Home Video Disc Rental Biz," *Variety*, July 25, 2013; Joan E. Solsman, "Verizon-Redbox Venture Advances," *The Wall Street Journal*, December 12, 2012; Kyle Stock, "Redbox Sacrifices Margins to Drive DVD Rentals," *Bloomberg Businessweek*, September 17, 2013.

Chapter 2

1. Thomas M. Burton and Serena Ng, "FDA Seeks Stricter Rules on Antibacterial Soaps," *The Wall Street Journal*, December 16, 2013; Brian Clark Howard, "Avoid Antibacterial Soaps, Say Consumer Advocates," *National Geographic*; Allison E. Aiello, Bonnie Marshall, Stuart B.

Levy, Phyllis Della-Latta, and Elaine Larson, "Relationship between Triclosan and Susceptibilities of Bacteria Isolated from Hands in Community," *Antimicrob Agents Chemother*, 48, no. 8 (2004), pp. 2973–79; Elizabeth Weise, "FDA: Antibacterial Soaps Could Pose Health Risks," *USA Today*, December 16, 2013; Andrew Martin, "Antibacterial Chemical Raises Safety Issues," *The New York Times*, August 19, 2011.

2. Kimberly Blanton, "Creating a Culture of Compliance," *CFO*, July/August 2011, pp. 19–21.
3. Better Business Bureau, "Origaudio"; Jenna Schnuer, "Emerging Entrepreneur of 2012: Jason Lucash," *Entrepreneur*, December 18, 2012; Jan Norman, "Fold Up Speakers Launch O.C. Company," *OC Register*, August 21, 2013; "The Foldable Speaker: The 50 Best Inventions of 2009," *Time*; OrigAudio website.
4. Kate Pickert, "Medicare Fraud Horror: Cancer Doctor Indicted for Billing Unnecessary Chemo," *Time*, August 15, 2013.
5. Ronald Alsop, "Corporate Scandals Hit Home," *The Wall Street Journal*, February 19, 2004.
6. Serena Ng and Joann S. Lublin, "Avon Raises Estimate of Bribery-Probe's Cost," *The Wall Street Journal*, February 14, 2014, p. B3.
7. O. C. Ferrell, John Fraedrich, and Linda Ferrell, *Business Ethics: Ethical Decision Making and Cases*, 8th ed. (Mason, OH: South-Western Cengage Learning, 2011), p. 7.
8. David Callahan, as quoted in Archie Carroll, "Carroll: Do We Live in a Cheating Culture?" *Athens Banner-Herald*, February 21, 2004.
9. Elliot Blair Smith and Phil Kuntz, "CEO Pay 1,795-to-1 Multiple of Wages Skirts the Law," *Bloomberg*, April 29, 2013.
10. Christopher Palmeri, "Disney's CEO Iger Sees Fiscal 2013 Compensation Slide 15%," *Bloomberg*, December 24, 2013.
11. Rick Jervis, "Guilty Verdict for Ex-Mayor Nagin Adds to Rubble of Katrina," *USA Today*, February 13, 2014, p. 2A.
12. The Editorial Board, "A-Rod's Drug Testing," *The New York Times*, January 19, 2014.
13. Ferrell, Fraedrich, and Ferrell, *Business Ethics*.
14. Ethics Resource Center, 2011 *National Business Ethics Survey®: Ethics in Transition* (Arlington, VA: Ethics Resource Center, 2012).
15. Bobby White, "The New Workplace Rules: No Video Watching," *The New York Times*, March 3, 2008, p. B1.
16. Shana Lebowitz, "What's Behind a Rise in Workplace Bullying?" *USA Today*, October 8, 2013.
17. Theodore V. Wells Jr., Brad S. Karp, Bruce Birenboim, and David W. Brown, *Report to the National Football League Concerning Issues of Workplace Conduct at the Miami Dolphins*, February 14, 2014.
18. Robert Ottinger, "No Such Thing as a Free Minute: City Employee Fired for Misusing Work Cellphone and What That Means for New York Workers," *NY Employment Lawyer*, June 30, 2013.
19. April Warren, "Man Who Misused Company Credit Card Sentenced to 240 Days in Jail," *Ocala Star Banner*, July 31, 2013.
20. "Proper Use of Company, Customer, and Supplier Resources," Boeing, November 19, 2001.
21. Barbara Kiviat, "A Bolder Approach to Credit-Agency Rating Reform," *Time*, September 18, 2009.
22. Christopher M. Matthews and John Carreyrou, "Ex-SAC Trader Found Guilty," *The Wall Street Journal*, February 7, 2014, A1–A2.
23. *Corruption Perceptions Index 2013*. Copyright Transparency International 2013. For more information, visit.
24. Matthew Garrett, "Your Best Employee Stinks and May Be Stealing From You," *Forbes*, October 1, 2013.
25. Associated Press, "EU Suspects 13 Banks of Collusion in Swaps Trading," *USA Today*, July 1, 2013.
26. Federal Trade Commission, "Nation's Largest Pool Products Distributor Settles FTC Charges of Anticompetitive Tactics," November 21, 2011.
27. Brady Dennis, "Trans Fats to Be Phased Out, FDA Says," *Washington Post*, November 7, 2013.
28. Josephson Institute, "The Ethics of American Youth: 2012," November 20, 2012.
29. Tom Vanden Hook, "Kickback Scandal Rocks Army," *USA Today*, February 4, 2014, p. 1A; Helene Cooper, "92 Air Force Officers Suspended for Cheating on Their Missile Exam," *The New York Times*, January 30, 2014; Kevin Liptak, "U.S. Navy Discloses Nuclear Exam Cheating," CNN, February 4, 2014; Julian E. Barnes, "Military Makes Ethics a Priority," *The Wall Street Journal*, February 3, 2014, p. A4.
30. James R. Healey and Fred Meier, "GM Knew about Cobalt Ignition Fault, Suit Says," *USA Today*, February 19, 2014, p. 1A; Alex Rogers, "GM Announces Another Major Recall Before Testimony," *Time*, March 31, 2013.
31. "Campaign Warns about Drugs from Canada," *CNN*, February 5, 2004; Gardiner Harris and Monica Davey, "FDA Begins Push to End Drug Imports," *The New York Times*, January 23, 2004, p. C1.
32. Lara Salahi, "FDA Appeals Block on Cigarette Warning Label," *ABC News*, November 30, 2011.
33. Ethics Resource Center, *2005 National Business Ethics Survey* (Washington, DC: Ethics Resource Center, 2005), p. 43.
34. Thomas M. Jones, "Ethical Decision Making by Individuals in Organizations: An Issue-Contingent Model," *Academy of Management Review* 2 (April 1991), pp. 371–73.
35. Sir Adrian Cadbury, "Ethical Managers Make Their Own Rules," *Harvard Business Review* 65 (September–October 1987), p. 72.
36. Chad Bray, "Perfume, Dresses and Cash in Ralph Lauren Bribe Scheme," *The Wall Street Journal*, April 22, 2013; Foreign Corrupt Practices Act; Peter Lattman, "Ralph Lauren Corp

Agrees to Pay Fine in Bribery Case," *The New York Times*, April 22, 2013.
37. Ferrell, Fraedrich, and Ferrell, *Business Ethics*, pp. 174–75.
38. Ethics Resource Center, *2009 National Business Ethics Survey* (Washington, DC: Ethics Resource Center, 2009), p. 41.
39. Texas Instruments, "Texas Instruments Rated One of the 'World's Most Ethical Companies' by Ethisphere Institute," March 6, 2013.
40. Ethics Resource Center, *2013 National Business Ethics Survey® of the U.S. Workforce* (Arlington, VA: Ethics Resource Center, 2014).
41. Ferrell, Fraedrich, and Ferrell, *Business Ethics*, p. 13.
42. "Trust in the Workplace: 2010 Ethics & Workplace Survey," Deloitte LLP (n.d.).
43. Archie B. Carroll, "The Pyramid of Corporate Social Responsibility: Toward the Moral Management of Organizational Stakeholders," *Business Horizons* 34 (July/August 1991), p. 42.
44. Kelly Kennedy, "Pharmacies Look to Snuff Tobacco Sales," *USA Today*, February 6, 2014, p. 1A.
45. Bryan Walsh, "Why Green Is the New Red, White and Blue," *Time*, April 28, 2008, p. 46.
46. Adam Shriver, "Not Grass-Fed, But at Least Pain-Free," *The New York Times*, February 18, 2010.
47. Alan Beattie, "Countries Rush to Restrict Trade in Basic Foods," *Financial Times*, April 2, 2008, p. 1.
48. PR Newswire, "Next Generation Philips 75 & 100 Watt LED Equivalents Achieve ENERGY STAR Certification and Could Sell for $10–15 After Rebates," February 18, 2014.
49. Cone Communications, "Cone Releases 2013 Cone Communications Green Gap Trend Tracker," April 2, 2013.
50. "2014 World's Most Ethical Companies—Honorees," *Ethisphere*.
51. Indra Nooyi, "The Responsible Company," *The Economist, The World in 2008 Special Edition*, March 2008, p. 132.
52. Ferrell, Fraedrich, and Ferrell, *Business Ethics*, pp. 13–19.
53. Abha Bhattarai, "Union Approves Contract with Safeway, Giant," *Washington Post*, December 22, 2013.
54. U.S. Equal Employment Opportunity Commission, "Ruby Tuesday Will Pay $575,000 to Resolve EEOC Class Age Discrimination Lawsuit," December 9, 2013.
55. Alan Zibel and Robin Sidel, "AmEx to Pay $76 Million in Car 'Add-On' Settlement," *The Wall Street Journal*, December 26, 2013, p. C3.
56. Todd Littman, "Win-Win Emissions Reductions Strategies," Victoria Transport Policy Institute.
57. Cornelia Dean, "Drugs Are in the Water, Does It Matter?" *The New York Times*, April 3, 2007.
58. Chris Woodyard, "Lighter Cars Add Weight to Repair," USA Today, September 16, 2013, 1B; Automotive News, "Adhesives Tapped to Make Cars Lighter," *Europe Auto News*, June 8, 2013; Brad Plumer, "Why Cars Will Keep Getting Lighter," *Washington Post*, January 12, 2012.
59. "Amazon Rainforest Deforestation at Lowest in 23 Years, Brazil Government Says," *Reuters*, December 5, 2011.
60. "Few State Laws Restrict Plastic Bags," *International New York Times*, May 18, 2013.
61. Josie Huang, "LA to Become Biggest City to Ban Plastic Bags on Jan. 1," *Southern California Public Radio*, December 24, 2013.
62. Brian Dumaine, "Brighter Days for First Solar," *CNN Money*, May 6, 2013.
63. "San Diego Hotel Makes Smart Sustainable Changes to Save Energy & Money," SDGE, September 5, 2013.
64. Adam Minter, "U.S. Isn't Flooding the Third World With E-Waste," *Bloomberg View*, May 26, 2013.
65. "GreenChoice Program Details," Austin Energy (n.d.).
66. "Certification," Home Depot.
67. Chiquita, Bananalink.
68. GE Foundation, "United Way".
69. Blue Smoke Coffee website.
70. Bureau of Labor Statistics, "Labor Force Statistics from the Current Population Survey.
71. Clare Kane, "Spain PM Sees Hope for Unemployment on Day of Protests," *Reuters*, June 1, 2013.
72. Andrea Hsu, "Iowa Town Braces for New Reality in Factory Closure's Wake," *NPR*, April 8, 2013.
73. Peter Cappelli, "Why Companies Aren't Getting the Employees They Need," *The Wall Street Journal*, October 24, 2011, pp. R1, R6.
74. "Create Jobs for USA Supporters"; "Starbucks and Opportunity Finance Network: Taking Action to Reduce Unemployment in America," *Huffington Post*, February 5, 2013.
75. "The Boston Consulting Group," *CNN Money*, February 4, 2013; "100 Best Companies to Work For," *CNNMoney*.
76. "Who Really Pays for CSR Initiatives," *Environmental Leader*, February 15, 2008; "Global Fund"; Reena Jana, "The Business of Going Green," *BusinessWeek Online*, June 22, 2007.
77. Permission granted by the author of *Gray Matters*, George Sammet Jr., Vice President, Office of Corporate Ethics, Lockheed Martin Corporation, Orlando, Florida, to use these portions of *Gray Matters: The Ethics Game* © 1992.
78. Edelman, *Edelman Trust Barometer*, 2012; "Occupying the Future: Benefit Corporations Now Opening Shop in NY, Six Other States," *Daily Kos*, December 14, 2011; Jessica Silver-Greenberg, Tara Kalwarski, and Alexis Leondis, "CEO Pay Drops, But . . . Cash Is King," *Bloomberg Businessweek*, April 5, 2010, pp. 50–56; "The Dynamics of Public Trust in Business—Emerging Opportunities for Leaders," Business Roundtable Institute for Corporate Ethics.
79. M. P. McQueen, "Agency Misses Chance to Curb Lead in Jewelry," *The Wall Street Journal*, February 12, 2008, p. D1.
80. Bart Jansen, "Justice Settles Merger Lawsuit with AA, US Airways," *USA*

Today, November 12, 2013.

81. Chad Bray, "Marvel Wins in Dispute Over Characters," *The Wall Street Journal*, August 8, 2013; U.S. Copyright Office, "Definitions"; Michael Cieply, "Disney Wins Marvel Copyright Case," *The New York Times*, July 28, 2011.
82. Maureen Dorney, "Congress Passes Federal Anti-Spam Law: Preempts Most State Anti-Spam Laws," *DLA Piper*, December 3, 2003,
83. Elizabeth Alterman, "As Kids Go Online, Identity Theft Claims More Victims," *CNBC*, October 10, 2011.
84. Federal Trade Commission, "Path Social Networking App Settles FTC Charges It Deceived Consumers and Improperly Collected Personal Information from Users' Mobile Address Books," February 1, 2013.
85. Jean Eaglesham and Ashby Jones, "Whistle-blower Bounties Pose Challenges," *The Wall Street Journal*, December 13, 2010, pp. C1, C3.
86. "Office of Financial Research," U.S. Department of Treasury; "Initiatives: Financial Stability Oversight Council," U.S. Department of Treasury.

Chapter 3

1. Simon Montlake and Ryan Ma, "China's Steve Jobs," *Forbes*, July 18, 2012; Laura He, "Chinese Billionaire Lei Jun and His iPhone Challenger Jump Into Fierce Smartphone Price War," *Forbes*, August 15, 2012; Hannah Beech/Chengdu, "The Cult of Apple in China," *Time*, July 2, 2012; Matt Schiavenza, "How Xiaomi's Hip, Inexpensive Smart Phones Conquered China," *The Atlantic*, October 24, 2013; Mark Milian, "China Loves Xiaomi Phones. Will Anyone Else?" *Bloomberg Technology*, January 5, 2014.
2. Tim Kelly, "Squash the Caterpillar," *Forbes*, April 21, 2008, p. 136.
3. Subway, "Explore Our World".
4. Deloitte, "2013 Global Manufacturing Competitiveness Index," 2013.
5. Seeking Alpha, "Starbucks' CEO Discusses F4Q 2013 Results—Earnings Call Transcript," *Yahoo! Finance*, October 30, 2013.
6. Elisabeth Sullivan, "Choose Your Words Wisely," *Marketing News*, February 15, 2008, p. 22.
7. UPI, "Apple Store in 2013 Hit $10 Billion Mark in App Sales," January 7, 2014; Alex Williams, "Apple Reports Q4 Retail Sales of $4.5 Billion with $50 Million in Sales per Apple Store," *Tech Crunch*, October 28, 2013.
8. Statista, "Total Population in the United States from 2003 to 2013 (in millions)," 2013.
9. Sullivan, "Choose Your Words Wisely."
10. Stephan Faris, "How Poland Became Europe's Most Dynamic Economy," *Bloomberg Businessweek*, November 27, 2013.
11. Tim Worstall, "Which Should We Have: Public Utilities or Regulated Private Monopolies?" *Forbes*, March 24, 2013.
12. Danielz Pylypczak, "Mexico Takes Steps to End Oil Monopoly," *Commodity HQ*, August 15, 2013.
13. T. S., "Why Does Kenya Lead the World in Mobile Money?" *The Economist*, May 27, 2013.
14. Paul Davidson, "We Produce More at Home with New Drilling Methods," *USA Today*, February 11, 2014, p. 1B.
15. Rosalie C. Periabras, "Philippines: The New Call Center Capital of the World," *The Manila Times*, October 26, 2013.
16. U.S. Bureau of the Census, Foreign Trade Division, *U.S. Trade in Goods and Services—Balance of Payments (BOP) Basis*, February 6, 2014.
17. Colum Murphy and Mike Ramsey, "Tesla Plans to Add Charging Network in China," *The Wall Street Journal*, January 15, 2014, p. B6; Daisuke Wakabayashi, Lorraine Luk, Ian Sherr, and Paul Mozur, "Apple Nears Major Expansion," *The Wall Street Journal*, September 7 –8, 2014, p. B1.
18. U.S. Bureau of the Census, Foreign Trade Division, *U.S. Trade in Goods and Services—Balance of Payments (BOP) Basis*, February 6, 2014.
19. Ibid.
20. Keith Bradsher, "G.M. Plans to Develop Electric Cars With China," *The New York Times*, September 20, 2011.
21. Fortune Industry Perspectives and Dupont, "Sustainable Energy for Growing China," May 2013; Josh Bateman, "The New Global Leader in Renewable Energy," *RenewableEnergyWorld.Com*, January 13, 2014; Wayne Ma, "China Boosts Renewable-Energy Surcharge," *The Wall Street Journal*, August 30, 2013.
22. Richard Silk, "Yuan's Climb Adds to Chinese Export Woes," *The Wall Street Journal*, January 11–12, 2014, p. A7.
23. Shelly Banjo and R. Jai Krishna, "Wal-Mart Curbs Ambitions in India," *The Wall Street Journal*, October 10, 2013, pp. B1–B2; Loretta Chao and Paulo Trevisani, "Brazil Presses on Internet Bill," *The Wall Street Journal*, November 19, 2013, p. B4; Brazilia, "Brazil Delays Vote on Anti-Spying Internet Bill-Lawmaker," *Reuters*, December 4, 2013.
24. Kurt Badenhausen, "Ireland Heads Forbes' List of the Best Countries for Business," *Forbes*, December 4, 2013.
25. "The Restricted Zone in Mexico," Penner & Associates—Mexico Law Firm and Business Consulting for Mexico.
26. "Sixth Annual BSA and IDC Global Software Piracy Study," Business Software Alliance, May 2009.
27. "USA: President Obama Should Take the Lead on Lifting Embargo against Cuba," Amnesty International, September 2, 2009; Kitty Bean Yancey, "Back to Cuba: 'People-to-People Trips' Get the Green Light," *USA Today*, August 4, 2011, p. 4A.
28. Kitty Bean Yancey and Laura Bly, "Door May Be Inching Open for Tourism," *USA Today*, February 20, 2008, p. A5; Sue Kirchhoff and Chris Woodyard, "Cuba Trade Gets 'New Opportunity,' " *USA Today*, February 20, 2008, p. B1.
29. Daniel Trotta, "U.S. Charges Five in 'Honeygate' Anti-Dumping Probe," *Reuters*, February 20, 2013.
30. Ibid.

31. Chris Huber, "Five of the Worst Natural Disasters in 2013," *World Vision*, December 19, 2013.
32. Julie Jargon, "Burger King Heads to India—Finally," *The Wall Street Journal*, November 20, 2013, p. B9.
33. Laurie Burkitt, "Tiffany Finds Sparkle in Overseas Markets," *The Wall Street Journal*, December 26, 2013, p. B4.
34. Julie Jargon, "Starbucks Shifts in Europe," *The Wall Street Journal*, November 30–December 1, 2013, p. B3.
35. "Slogans Gone Bad," Joe-ks.
36. Preetika Rana, "Ad Confronts Taboos for Women in India," *The Wall Street Journal*, November 20, 2013, p. A8.
37. J. Bonasia, "For Web, Global Reach Is Beauty—and Challenge," *Investor's Business Daily*, June 13, 2001, p. A6.
38. Chuck Jones, "PC Market Consolidating Around Top 3 Vendors," *Forbes*, October 10, 2013; Jason Evangelho, "2013 Represented Worst Decline in PC Market's History," *Forbes*, January 9, 2014.
39. Heidi Vogt, "Startup Keeps Africa's Jet Set Aloft," *The Wall Street Journal*, August 16, 2013; Travel Pulse, "World Economic Forum Honors TanJet Founder Mashibe," Travel Pulse, Marche 21, 2011; Jacey Fortin, "African Air Travel: Why Are Airlines in Africa So Expensive, Unsafe and Impossible to Navigate," *IBT Media*, May 4, 2013.
40. "What Is the WTO," World Trade Organization (n.d.).
41. World Trade Organization, "Argentina Files Dispute against the European Union over Biodiesel," December 20, 2013.
42. "North American Free Trade Agreement," NAFTANOW.ORG, April 4, 2012.
43. Central Intelligence Agency, "Country Comparison: GDP—Per Capital (PPP)," *The CIA World Factbook*.
44. Executive Office of the President of the United States, "U.S.–Canada Trade Facts".
45. Trading Economics, "Canada Exports"; Executive Office of the President of the United States, "U.S.–Canada Trade Facts."
46. "America's Biggest Partners," *CNBC.com*.
47. Central Intelligence Agency, "Country Comparison: GDP—Per Capital (PPP)."
48. Executive Office of the President of the United States, "U.S.–Mexico Trade Facts".
49. Jen Wieczner, "Why 2014 Could Be Mexico's Year," *Fortune*, January 13, 2014, pp. 37–38.
50. "A Tale of Two Mexicos: North and South," *The Economist*, April 26, 2008, pp. 53–54.
51. United States Census Bureau, "Top Trading Partners—December 2013: Year-to-Date Total Trade".
52. Pete Engardio and Geri Smith, "Business Is Standing Its Ground," *BusinessWeek*, April 20, 2009, pp. 34–39.
53. "Europe in 12 Lessons".
54. Central Intelligence Agency, "Country Comparison: GDP (Official Exchange Rate)," *The CIA World Factbook.*
55. Stanley Reed, with Ariane Sains, David Fairlamb, and Carol Matlack, "The Euro: How Damaging a Hit?" *BusinessWeek*, September 29, 2003, p. 63; "The Single Currency," CNN (n.d.).
56. Claire Cain Miller, "Google Settles Its European Antitrust Case; Critics Remain," *International New York Times*, February 5, 2014.
57. Abigail Moses, "Greek Contagion Concern Spurs European Sovereign Default Risk to Record," *Bloomberg*, April 26, 2010.
58. James G. Neuger and Joe Brennan, "Ireland Weighs Aid as EU Spars over Debt-Crisis Remedy," *Bloomberg*.
59. Charles Forelle and Marcus Walker, "Dithering at the Top Turned EU Crisis to Global Threat," *The Wall Street Journal*, December 29, 2011, p. A1; Jeff Cox, "US, Europe Face More Ratings Cuts in Coming Years," CNBC, January 20, 2012; Charles Forelle, "Greece Defaults and Tries to Move On," *The Wall Street Journal*, March 10, 2012.
60. Kiran Moodley, "S&P Cuts Netherlands Rating; Cyprus and Spain Seen More Positive," *CNBC*, November 29, 2013.
61. "Powerhouse Deutschland," *Bloomberg Businessweek*, January 3, 2011, p. 93; Alan S. Blinder, "The Euro Zone's German Crisis," The Wall Street Journal.
62. "About APEC".
63. "China Economic Growth Rate Stabilises at 7.7%," *BBC News*, January 20, 2014.
64. Charles Riley and Feng Ke, "China to Overtake U.S. as World's Top Trader," *CNN*, January 10, 2014.
65. U.S. Environmental Protection Agency, "Global Greenhouse Gas Emissions Data"; Joshua Keating, "China Passes U.S. as World's Largest Oil Importer," *Slate*, October 11, 2013.
66. Jayne O'Donnell and Calum Macleod, "Bangladesh Fire Ads Pressure on Retailers," *USA Today*, May 10, 2013, p. 1B; Anne D'Innocenzio, "Companies Adopt Safety Plan for Bangladesh Factories," *Boston Globe*, July 9, 2013; Steven Greenhouse, "As Firms Line Up on Factories, Wal-Mart Plans Solo Effort," *The New York Times*, May 14, 2013.
67. Charles Riley, "Starbucks to Open First Store in Vietnam," *CNN*, January 3, 2013.
68. "Overview," Association of Southeast Asian Nations.
69. Wang Yan, "ASEAN Works to 'Act as Unison' on Global Stage," *China Daily*, November 19, 2011.
70. ASEAN website.
71. "Agreement on the Common Effective Preferential Tariff (CEPT) Scheme for the ASEAN Free Trade Area (AFTA)," Association of Southeast Asian Nations.
72. R.C., "No Brussels Sprouts in Bali," *The Economist*, November 18, 2011.
73. Eric Bellman, "Asia Seeks Integration Despite EU's Woes," *The Wall Street Journal*, July 22, 2011, p. A9.
74. David J. Lynch, "The IMF is . . . Tired Fund Struggles to Reinvent Itself," *USA Today*, April 19, 2006. p. B1.
75. Walter B. Wriston, "Ever Heard of Insourcing?" Commentary, *The Wall*

Street Journal, March 24, 2004, p. A20.

76. "Here, There and Everywhere," A Special Report, *The Economist*, January 19, 2013, pp. 1–20.
77. Nick Heath, "Banks: Offshoring, Not Outsourcing," *BusinessWeek*, March 10, 2009.
78. Panos Mourdoukoutas, "How GM Wins in China," *Forbes*, February 19, 2013.
79. PR Newswire, "PKO Bank Polski and EVO Payments International Finalize Sale of 66 Percent of eService Shares and Creation of a 20 Year Strategic Alliance," January 8, 2014.
80. Nokia Corporation, "Nokia to Fully Acquire Siemens' Stake in Nokia Siemens Network," July 1, 2013.
81. Guo Changdong and Ren Ruqin, "Nestle CEO visits Tianjin," *China Daily*, August 12, 2010; "Employee Profiles," Nestlé.
82. O. C. Ferrell, John Fraedrich, and Linda Ferrell, *Business Ethics*, 6th ed. (Boston: Houghton Miffl in, 2005), pp. 227–30.
83. Vu Trong Khanh, "Vietnam Gets Its First McDonald's," *The Wall Street Journal*, February 11, 2014, p. B4.
84. Export.gov; CIBER Web.
85. Zachary-Cy Vanasse, "Rendez Vous En France Brings the World Travel Industry to Paris," *Travel Hot News*, April 5, 2012; Malcolm Moore, "Disney Breaks Ground on Shanghai Theme Park," *The Telegraph*, April 8, 2011; Jeff Chu, "Happily Ever After?" *Time*, March 18, 2002; Wendy Leung, "Disney Set to Miss Mark on Visitors," *The Standard*, September 5, 2006; Robert Mendick, "Race Against Time to Make That Disney Magic Work," *The London Independent*, February 6, 2000; "The Narrative of Numbers," Disneyland Paris.

Glossary 术语表

A

absolute advantage a monopoly that exists when a country is the only source of an item, the only producer of an item, or the most efficient producer of an item.

Asia-Pacific Economic Cooperation (APEC) an international trade alliance that promotes open trade and economic and technical cooperation among member nations.

Association of Southeast Asian Nations (ASEAN) A trade alliance that promotes trade and economic integration among member nations in Southeast Asia.

B

balance of payments the difference between the flow of money into and out of a country.

balance of trade the difference in value between a nation's exports and its imports.

bribes payments, gifts, or special favors intended to influence the outcome of a decision.

budget deficit the condition in which a nation spends more than it takes in from taxes.

business individuals or organizations who try to earn a profit by providing products that satisfy people's needs.

business ethics principles and standards that determine acceptable conduct in business.

C

capitalism (free enterprise) an economic system in which individuals own and operate the majority of businesses that provide goods and services.

cartel a group of firms or nations that agrees to act as a monopoly and not compete with each other, in order to generate a competitive advantage in world markets.

codes of ethics formalized rules and standards that describe what a company expects of its employees.

communism first described by Karl Marx as a society in which the people, without regard to class, own all the nation's resources.

comparative advantage the basis of most international trade, when a country specializes in products that it can supply more efficiently or at a lower cost than it can produce other items.

competition the rivalry among businesses for consumers' dollars.

consumerism the activities that independent individuals, groups, and organizations undertake to protect their rights as consumers.

contract manufacturing the hiring of a foreign company to produce a specified volume of the initiating company's product to specification; the final product carries the domestic firm's name.

corporate citizenship the extent to which businesses meet the legal, ethical, economic, and voluntary responsibilities placed on them by their stakeholders.

countertrade agreements foreign trade agreements that involve bartering products for other products instead of for currency.

D

demand the number of goods and services that consumers are willing to buy at different prices at a specific time.

depression a condition of the economy in which unemployment is very high, consumer spending is low, and business output is sharply reduced.

direct investment the ownership of overseas facilities.

dumping the act of a country or business selling products at less than what it costs to produce them.

E

economic contraction a slowdown of the economy characterized by a decline in spending and during which businesses cut back on production and lay off workers.

economic expansion the situation that occurs when an economy is growing and people are spending more money; their purchases stimulate the production of goods and services, which in turn stimulates employment.

economic system a description of how a particular society distributes its resources to produce goods and services.

economics the study of how resources are distributed for the production of goods and services within a social system.

embargo a prohibition on trade in a particular product.

entrepreneur an individual who risks his or her wealth, time, and effort to develop for profit an innovative product or way of doing something.

equilibrium price the price at which the number of products that businesses are willing to supply equals the amount of products that consumers are willing to buy at a specific point in time.

ethical issue an identifiable problem, situation, or opportunity that requires a person to choose from among several actions that may be evaluated as right or wrong, ethical or unethical.

European Union (EU) a union of European nations established in 1958 to promote trade among its members; one of the largest single markets today.

exchange controls regulations that restrict the amount of currency that can be bought or sold.

exchange rate the ratio at which one nation's currency can be exchanged for another nation's currency.

exporting the sale of goods and services to foreign markets.

F

financial resources the funds used to acquire the natural and human resources needed to provide products; also called capital.

franchising a form of licensing in which a company—the franchiser—agrees to provide a franchisee a name, logo, methods of operation, advertising, products, and other elements associated with a franchiser's business in return for a financial commitment and the agreement to conduct business in accordance with the franchiser's standard of operations.

free-market system pure capitalism, in which all economic decisions are made without government intervention.

G

General Agreement on Tariffs and Trade (GATT) a trade agreement, originally signed by 23 nations in 1947, that provided a forum for tariff negotiations and a place where international trade problems could be discussed and resolved.

global strategy (globalization) a strategy that involves standardizing products (and, as much as possible, their promotion and distribution) for the whole world, as if it were a single entity.

gross domestic product (GDP) the sum of all goods and services produced in a country during a year.

H

human resources the physical and mental abilities that people use to produce goods and services; also called labor.

I

import tariff a tax levied by a nation on goods imported into the country.

importing the purchase of goods and services from foreign sources.

inflation a condition characterized by a continuing rise in prices.

infrastructure the physical facilities that support a country's economic activities, such as railroads, highways, ports, airfields, utilities and power plants, schools, hospitals, communication systems, and commercial distribution systems.

international business the buying, selling, and trading of goods and services across national boundaries.

International Monetary Fund (IMF) organization established in 1947 to promote trade among member nations by eliminating trade barriers and fostering financial cooperation.

J

joint venture a partnership established for a specific project or for a limited time.

L

licensing a trade agreement in which one company—the licensor—allows another company—the licensee—to use its company name, products, patents, brands, trademarks, raw materials, and/or production processes in exchange for a fee or royalty.

M

mixed economies economies made up of elements from more than one economic system.

monopolistic competition the market structure that exists when there are fewer businesses than in a purecompetition environment and the differences among the goods they sell are small.

monopoly the market structure that exists when there is only one business providing a product in a given market.

multinational corporation (MNC) a corporation that operates on a worldwide scale, without significant ties to any one nation or region.

multinational strategy a plan, used by international companies, that involves customizing products, promotion, and distribution according to cultural, technological, regional, and national differences.

N

natural resources land, forests, minerals, water, and other things that are not made by people.

nonprofit organizations organizations that may provide goods or services but do not have the fundamental purpose of earning profits.

North American Free Trade Agreement (NAFTA) agreement that eliminates most tariffs and trade restrictions on agricultural and manufactured products to encourage trade among Canada, the United States, and Mexico.

O

offshoring the relocation of business processes by a company or subsidiary to another country. Offshoring is different than outsourcing because the company retains control of the offshored processes.

oligopoly the market structure that exists when there are very few businesses selling a product.

outsourcing the transferring of manufacturing or other tasks—such as data processing—to countries where labor and supplies are less expensive.

P

plagiarism the act of taking someone else's work and presenting it as your own without mentioning the source.

product a good or service with tangible and intangible characteristics that provide satisfaction and benefits.

profit the difference between what it costs to make and sell a product and what a customer pays for it.

pure competition the market structure that exists when there are many small businesses selling one standardized product.

Q

quota a restriction on the number of units of a particular product that can be imported into a country.

R

recession a decline in production, employment, and income.

S

social responsibility a business's obligation to maximize its positive impact and minimize its negative impact on society.

socialism an economic system in which the government owns and operates basic industries but individuals own most businesses.

stakeholders groups that have a stake in the success and outcomes of a business.

strategic alliance a partnership formed to create competitive advantage on a worldwide basis.

supply the number of products—goods and services—that businesses are willing to sell at different prices at a specific time.

sustainability conducting activities in a way that allows for the long-term well-being of the natural environment, including all biological entities; involves the assessment and improvement of business strategies, economic sectors, work practices, technologies, and lifestyles so that they maintain the health of the natural environment.

T

trade deficit a nation's negative balance of trade, which exists when that country imports more products than it exports.

trading company a firm that buys goods in one country and sells them to buyers in another country.

U

unemployment the condition in which a percentage of the population wants to work but is unable to find jobs.

W

whistleblowing the act of an employee exposing an employer's wrongdoing to outsiders, such as the media or government regulatory agencies.

World Bank an organization established by the industrialized nations in 1946 to loan money to underdeveloped and developing countries; formally known as the International Bank for Reconstruction and Development.

World Trade Organization (WTO) international organization dealing with the rules of trade between nations.

Photo Credits 图片版权

Chapter 1 Opener (left): © McGraw-Hill Education/Mark A.S. Dierker, photographer; Opener (right): © McGraw-Hill Education/Jill Braaten, photographer; p. 5: © McGraw-Hill Education/Mark A.S. Dierker, photographer; p. 7: © PRNewsFoto/AP Photos; p. 9: Courtesy of Young Americans Center for Financial Education; p. 11: © Paul J. Richards/AFP/Getty Images; p. 13: © Purestock/SuperStock; p. 23: © PC Plus Magazine/Getty Images; p. 24: © Ariel Skelley/Getty Images.

Chapter 2 Opener: © McGraw-Hill Education/Mark A.S. Dierker, photographer; p. 39: © Joe Kohen/Getty Images; p. 40: © NC1 WENN Photos/Newscom; p. 41: © Richard Levine/Alamy; p. 45: © Jane Williams/Alamy; p. 46: © Onsite/Alamy; p. 47: © Chuck Solomon/Getty Images; p. 56: © Dave Sandford/Getty Images; p. 59: © Idealink Photography/Alamy; p. 61: © Julie Edwards/Alamy; p. 67: © John Ewing/Portland Press Herald via Getty Images; p. 76: © Onoky Photography/SuperStock.

Chapter 3 Opener: © ChinaFotoPress/Getty Images; p. 84: © China/Alamy; p. 85: © Qilai Shen/Bloomberg via Getty Images; p. 90: © McGraw-Hill Education/Christopher Kerrigan, photographer; p. 91: © Henri Conodul/Iconotec.com; p. 92: © Tetra Images/Getty Images; p. 95: © Joseph Van Os/Getty Images; p. 97: © scibak/iStock; p. 101: © Philip Scalia/Alamy; p. 105: © Walter Bibikow/Corbis; p. 106: © Li Jian/Xinhua/Photoshot/Newscom.